GOD, ENERGY AND THE FIELD

First published by O Books, 2008
O Books is an imprint of John Hunt Publishing Ltd., The Bothy, Deershot Lodge, Park Lane, Ropley,
Hants, SO24 0BE, UK
office1@o-books.net
www.o-books.net

Distribution in:	South Africa
	Alternative Books
UK and Europe	altbook@peterhyde.co.za
Orca Book Services	Tel: 021 555 4027 Fax: 021 447 1430
orders@orcabookservices.co.uk	
Tel: 01202 665432 Fax: 01202 666219 Int. code (44)	Text copyright Adrian B. Smith 2008
	Design: Stuart Davies
USA and Canada	
NBN	ISBN: 978 1 84694 135 1
custserv@nbnbooks.com	
Tel: 1 800 462 6420 Fax: 1 800 338 4550	All rights reserved. Except for brief quotations in critical articles or reviews, no part of this
Australia and New Zealand	book may be reproduced in any manner without
Brumby Books	prior written permission from the publishers.
sales@brumbybooks.com.au	
Tel: 61 3 9761 5535 Fax: 61 3 9761 7095	The rights of Adrian B. Smith as author have been asserted in accordance with the
Far East (offices in Singapore, Thailand, Hong Kong, Taiwan)	Copyright, Designs and Patents Act 1988.
Pansing Distribution Pte Ltd	
kemal@pansing.com	A CIP catalogue record for this book is available
Tel: 65 6319 9939 Fax: 65 6462 5761	from the British Library.

Printed in Great Britain by
CPI Antony Rowe, Chippenham, Wiltshire

GOD, ENERGY AND THE FIELD

Adrian B. Smith

BOOKS

Winchester, UK
Washington, USA

Do not look for God outside yourself, for the God which you seek does not exist.
God manifests in us as light in our spirit, sweet warmth in our heart,
and strength in our will.
Look within for the living God, and be thankful.

Ask that God may live in you, that He may manifest through you.
Only God can transform human beings.
Everyone is seeking the meaning of life.
The meaning of life lies in communion with God.

The Great Beings, Geniuses and Masters of Humanity are those in whom God lives.

God is the goal of life; it is He we are seeking.
God is the beloved of the human soul.

(Peter Deunov, 1864-1944. the great seer of Bulgaria)

CONTENTS

DEDICATION

I dedicate this book to the memory of Peter Levesley a soul-brother for thirty years and my partner for twelve years in leading the More-to-Life non-religious retreats, who left us for a better life in November 2006, having made the transition from an outer form of Christianity, expressed in Roman Catholicism, to an inner form experienced as a Quaker.

INTRODUCTION

Although this book stands on its own, it could be seen as a successor to a previous book – *The God Shift* - in which I examined thirteen factors in our contemporary life which are causing Christians to feel uneasy about the traditional concept of God and about some of the doctrines that flow from it.

In the Introduction to that book I warned that I was not offering an alternative perception of God, but simply a compass to assist each reader to choose their own spiritual path.

In this present book, however, I take the bold step of proposing that there might be a perception of the Ultimate Reality, expressed by that inadequately small but enormously evocative and emotionally charged word 'God', one which is more meaningful for our day, thus enabling the reader to acquire a new kind of relationship with God.

From the time our earliest ancestors emerged from primates to humans (Homo sapiens) becoming self-reflective creatures, with a sense of space and time, they experienced that there existed a power beyond their control, a transcendent reality which they called upon to achieve that which was beyond their ability. These gods took different forms in different cultures, but in each case the image was a human creation. Through thousands of years, these images became more and more refined in proportion as human beings understood their world.

The image of God as a transcendent Superlative-human, with which we in the West are most familiar, is that of the Judeo-Christian tradition. But since images change with the advances of human knowledge, no one image can be set in concrete for all time.

While God is completely beyond our intellectual comprehension, God is not beyond our experience or imagination. In the Middle Ages the German mystic Meister Eckhart made the distinction between God and the Godhead. The latter is way beyond our human comprehension but we need some way of relating to the Divine and so we create an image of a God who has all the human attributes to an 'nth' degree. We can do no other: as human beings, believing ourselves to be at the present peak of the evolutionary process, we are unable to conceive of a Being other than as a super human. And so we address God as Lord, Judge, King, Almighty, Creator.

In our own time the same distinction has been made by the Protestant theologian Paul Tillich (in *The Courage To Be*) writing of 'the God above God' as 'the object of all mystical longing'.

GOD MANIFEST AND UNMANIFEST

We find the same distinction made by Hindu teachers over two millennia ago who speak of God unmanifest, *Nirguna God*, the eternal self-existing divine reality, and God manifest, *Saguna God*. This latter is God in relation to His creation expressed with human attributes but to a superlative degree: personality, omniscience, goodness, love, omnipotence.

In this book I am not writing about God Unmanifest, the Godhead - indeed no one can, except to say 'the Godhead is not this, not that' (called apophatic philosopher Ludwig Feuerbach. He interpreted belief in God as a kind of concealed anthropology in which all the noble attributes of the human species are projected on to an imaginary being in the sky.

In Part One I define the terms in the title. In Part Two I explore some of the consequences for the Christian of perceiving God in this new way. I invite you to explore with me!

* * *

I wish to express my gratitude to those who have read the text and offered their ideas for its improvement and especially to Prof. Chris Clarke for assisting with the scientific content of chapters 2 and 3.

1. GOD

If you understand Him, He is not God
(St Augustine of Hippo)

It is difficult for us who live in the western world today to conceive of the fear that gripped our early ancestors, of the hold that fear had on their lives. Not simply instinctive fear, which we all inherit - fear of fire, fear of spiders, fear of the dark, fear of thunder. Nor even physical fear, which we also inherit which sends us a rush of adrenalin. These fears arise from our survival instinct to protect us from danger. But add to these a reasoned fear: a fear of attack by their enemies, a fear of being bewitched, of being poisoned by a rival. I have met this dominating fear among the rural people with whom I was living in Zambia. Then add to this list a fear of the elements. In our own technological society, it is only when faced with monumental natural disasters - tsunami, hurricanes, floods, drought - that we feel our impotence, but for everyday living we can cope with the elements. In Zambia the only tools the villagers had in order to survive in their environment, to enable the earth to produce their food, were a machete and a hoe and also fire. For the greater part they were reliant upon the blessings of their gods and the smile of their ancestors.

With our technology we rarely have to call upon a higher power to act on our behalf: 'God, quick, find me a parking space'!

With just a suspicion of what our earliest pre-technological ancestors must have had to face, to cope with survival, we can understand why Petronius, a first century Latin satirical writer wrote: 'It is fear that first brought gods into the world'.

These early ancestors were aware of a power, an energy greater than themselves which seemed to govern their lives from above. For their survival they needed to tap into this power. Conceiving of it in human terms, they related to it by gifts, bribery, sacrifice - even the supreme sacrifice of human blood.

DOES GOD EVOLVE?

While the Godhead does not evolve, the human image of the immanent God and the consequent way in which humanity has related to God, has evolved.

We can trace this progression through our own Judeo-Christian history, from belief in a plurality of gods, to the monotheism of the Hebrew prophets, to a Trinitarian God as defined in the fourth century of Christianity, to today's non-theistic, non-interventionist God of panentheism.

It is in the East that we find the earliest written records of religious belief, in the *Vedas*, those great Hindu writings, which date back to the fourth millennium BCE. They were, and are still, not simply intellectual accounts, but in the vibration of their mantras contain an energy which brings forth life. (Are we not reminded of the opening words of John's gospel describing life issuing from God's utterance: 'In the beginning was the word....' a vibration?)

Long before our earliest known Hebrew history, the story of Abraham, perhaps some 2000 years BCE, the

Egyptians had created a civilisation with their own understanding of the gods, which lasted for at least 3000 years. Some of the Hebrew psalms and parts of the Book of Proverbs are taken from the Egyptian dynasty and Arab wisdom.

The religions of the Egyptians, Hebrews, Greeks, Romans, Babylonians, Indians and Chinese all had this in common: that the Divine was situated in the sky above the Earth (which was not far away according to the cosmology of the time) and that everything earthly had its heavenly counterpart, while everything heavenly had its earthly counterpart. That close were the worlds of gods and humans. So we read in Genesis (6:1-4) 'When mankind was spread all over the world, and girls were being born, the sons of god saw that these girls were beautiful, so they married as many as they chose. There were giants on Earth who where descendants of human women and the supernatural beings.' (Is this reflected in the Annunciation story several millennia later?)

THE HEBREW STORY

For Abraham, the wandering shepherd, his god was one of many local gods, a house-god, carried from place to place as his group wandered in the desert. His was an intimate god named El with whom Abraham held conversations, a god who sometimes even appeared in human form as one or more men (Genesis 18: 22-33). The god of Moses, centuries later, was a fearsome character, but not yet omnipotent. Some of the 'miracles' that his god performed through Moses were trumped by Pharaoh's magicians. Nevertheless, a god of power, able to liberate the Hebrew slaves from Egypt against all odds. This is the god who formed a community of different tribes by uniting them with a common covenant. This is the god who gave them ten commandments which to this day form the basis of moral law in the West. (Incidentally, this was not the first written code. The code of Hammurabi, several dozen generations before Moses, was inscribed on a black basalt stele where it can be seen today in the Louvre Museum in Paris.)

God was still a tribal god, living among them in a tent as they wandered around in the desert, and later residing in Solomon's Temple in Jerusalem.

The next stage of God's 'growth' was when the Israelites were banished into exile in Babylon (after 587 BCE) their Temple having been destroyed. There they encountered the world view of the Persians who believed that there were two primordial forces constantly battling for control of the world. Thus was laid the foundation of our western dualism. It is said that the Israelites also met the concept of angels in Babylon and it was from there that they obtained the first notions of hell and heaven as places of punishment and reward. Other ideas which they first encountered in Persia concerned physical resurrection, the model of the Last Day and the vision of a messianic figure who would introduce a new age by overthrowing the Evil One.

THE GREAT LEAP

It was during what has come to be called the Axial Age (600-300 BCE), when there was a great leap in human consciousness, that polytheism gave way to monotheism. This was the period of the founders of the great religions: Gautama Buddha, Leo Tzu, Zoroaster, Confucius, as also of the Greek philosophers and the

Hebrew prophets. It saw the birth of philosophy, mathematics, music, the dawn of democracy and citizenship.

It is said that it was the Greeks who 'discovered' the secular. They discovered spheres of activity which were independent of religious conditions. Since then, we in the West have made a division in our lives between the sacred and the profane, the spiritual and the material, the religious and the secular and consequently labelled the former 'religion' as apart from the rest of life. It is the concept of God as held by each religion which dictates how its God is to be related to. Religion is not departmentalised in the East nor was it so in biblical times. There the God-element is intrinsically bound up with the whole of life. It is a philosophy of life, our way of explaining the most fundamental questions about life that have been with humanity ever since human beings were able to differentiate between other beings and themselves. Such questions as: 'Where did we come from? Does life have a purpose? Why is there suffering?' (It is on account of our distinguishing and labelling 'religion' as a department of life that some Christians mistakenly refer to Buddhists as atheists, because they do not relate to an image of God as we do.)

Right up to our own time we have had to create an image of a Supreme Being. We gave it a variety of names, none of which was remotely adequate. We thought of it as Super-human. As humans we could do no other. Xenophanes, a Greek philosopher wrote: 'Human beings think of gods as having been born, wearing clothes, speaking and having bodies like their own. Ethiopians say the gods are black with snub noses. Thracians say they have blue eyes and red hair.

If cows and horses had hands they would draw pictures of the gods looking like cows and horses.'

The attributes we ascribe to God, which we regard as human ideals, such as justice, love, peace, forgiveness, mercy, issue from our own inner depth. Our image of God is of necessity in close relationship with Earth, its creator, its sustainer, our destiny, even taking this to the point of believing that all else in the entire Universe during its 14 billion years was created because God ultimately wanted human beings 'to love Him and serve Him in this world and to be happy with Him for ever in the next' as I learnt from my catechism as a child.

A PARADIGM SHIFT

I believe that today, there is a fundamental shift in theological thinking coming about on account of a shift in the very foundation of Christian belief. This foundation is from Super-nature Theism to Panentheism. Super-nature Theism is that which understands God in the way God is traditionally regarded in the Bible and in Christian worship today. Namely, that a personified God operates from outside creation, intervening in the world's and humanity's affairs as the whim takes Him.* The God we label Panentheistic (from the Greek meaning everything in God, and consequently God in everything) acts from within creation.

Although Panentheism is a comparatively new word in Christian theology (it was coined as late as 1829 by the philosopher and mystic Karl Christian

---

* I use the capital H with He, Him, His for God as distinct from a gender "he".

Friedrich Krause) the concept is not. We find this way of thinking in Psalm 139 of the Hebrew Scriptures and in Acts 17: 28 when St Paul, in Athens, quotes a Greek poet (possibly Epimenides – 6thC BCE): 'in Him we live and move and have our being'.

The Oxford Dictionary of the Christian Church defines Panentheism as: 'The belief that the Being of God includes and penetrates the whole Universe, so that every part of it exists in Him, but (as against Pantheism) that His Being is more than and is not exhausted by the Universe.'

The mystics of the Middle Ages expressed this concept without naming it. 'The day of my spiritual awakening was the day I saw and knew I saw all things in God and God in all things.' (Mechtild of Magdeburg, 1210-1280). And a century later Nicholas of Cusa (1400-1464): 'Divinity is the enfolding and unfolding of everything that is. Divinity is in all things in such a way that all things are in Divinity.'

Many panentheistic theologians, failing to distinguish between God unmanifest and God manifest have a problem with the word 'in'. Since God unmanifest cannot have special attributes, the 'in' expresses an intimacy of relationship – God manifest. There is evil and sin in the world. God cannot be in that, so He cannot be in everything nor can evil and sin be in God. In regarding God, as I do here, as manifest in energy – there is only one (good) energy – we overcome this difficulty. There is no such thing as negative energy, only energy misused (as I shall develop in a later chapter) and that is only by us. Of all creation, human beings alone are the cause of evil because we alone have the free will to choose our actions. While it is true that higher species of animals appear to have a sense of self-awareness, it only fully unfolds in the human mind. It is this quality of self-awareness that gives us an ability to make choices.

AN INTERVENTIONIST GOD

The inadequacy of our imaging God as a super model of ourselves is simply not satisfying in today's total picture. Belief in an interventionist God causes us to ask such questions as why He allows natural disasters such as the tsunami, a drought, a flood; why are some people chosen to be rescued while others are allowed to perish; why is this young person taken in her prime, and another have to endure a prolonged agonising death? Why indeed does a good God allow us to suffer? Does God have favourites?

When Jesus spoke of his relationship with God he could only describe it in human terms: 'I and the Father are one'. That is not said by someone on Earth relating to Someone 'up there' in heaven. His is not the relationship of a creature to a creator, of child to parent, of son to father (despite the designation). It is the relationship of his humanity with God here and now. Jesus did not have moments of ecstasy in which he was drawn up to the seventh heaven of St Paul, but continually lived the experience of unity consciousness with the creative God working through him in his daily life.

Gregory Baum wrote: 'God is not an object of which man may have an observer knowledge. Why? Because God is present in the very man who knows God and in the very process of knowing God' (*Man Becoming*).

We need a third way between the inaccessible, transcendent Godhead and the immanent human-like Father God: the next stage in God's 'growth'. We need to let go of images, to start from our human experience. We need a new name for God. 'Man's last and highest parting occurs when, for God's sake, he takes leave of God', wrote Meister Eckhart.

Today our knowledge has been expanded. The very vastness of the Universe is beyond our imagining. We recognise that time and space are elements of creation, that in the sub-atomic field effects can come about without a cause, that everything in the Universe is in perpetual motion, nothing is still, everything is in constant change.

Where, we ask, does the energy, the power driving this evolution come from? Not, as we have said, from a Being above, outside the Universe, but from an influence, a power, within.

This idea goes back a long way. During the early Christian and Byzantine periods the Greek patristic authors employed the words 'essence' and 'energy' to articulate the double truth of God as transcendent yet immanent. In His 'essence' God is infinitely transcendent (unmanifest), utterly beyond all created being, beyond all understanding and beyond all participation from the human side. But in His 'energies' God is inexhaustibly immanent, maintaining all creation in being – he is 'making' the world – and animating everything.

The essence-energy distinction goes back at least as far as the 1st century Jewish author Philo of Alexandria. It is taken from Philo by Clement of Alexandria (150-215). St Athanasius of Alexandria (295-373) wrote: 'God is in essence outside the Universe but He is present in everything through His acts of power' (His energy).

Divine energies are not an intermediary between

God and humanity, not a 'thing' that exists apart from God. They are, on the contrary, God Himself, God in action, God in His self-revelation, God indwelling His creation through His direct and unmediated presence. Meister Eckhart, in the 14th century, commented in an imaginative way: 'What does God do all day long? God lies in a maternity bed giving birth'.

God is manifest as the creative energy. Or to put it another way, God manifest is energy. So let's have a look at energy.

2. ENERGY

If we are to welcome into our lives a God image that is more real in our times than the Sky God, then it will be a model based upon what we know of our Universe, for there is no way we can have any concept of a Divine Being beyond the Universe. The Universe contains the sum total of all we know, all we can know. God Manifest can only be manifest through His creation. Any image we create of God Manifest can only issue from our human consciousness.

Underlying everything in the Universe is energy. Energy is the prime reality. Energy is the foundation of everything in the Universe from the minute atom to the mighty galaxy. Everything in the Universe, at whatever level, whether human, living, inorganic, stellar, or atomic is therefore connected to everything else through energy. Ultimately, it seems that all energy is one; that there is only one energy though its manifestations are numerous and it causes different effects. It is the great unifier of everything in our Universe. It is through energy that everything in creation is inter-related and inter-dependent. . In this chapter I will speak of energy, in the next about the way it acts through the effects of a universal field.

WHAT IS ENERGY?
So, what is energy? Put simply, we can say it is the principle of change. In our present context we can say

that it is the creative factor which holds all creation in an evolving existence. But what is its essential nature? We just do not know. Since nobody has yet come up with a definitive answer, the best we can do is to acknowledge the ways in which energy manifests itself.

It manifests itself in a variety of forms. In fact these are remarkably diverse. For the physicists, the core sense of energy is energy of motion, Kinetic Energy, which is a measure of how much force is required to set an object in motion, or to bring it to rest, over a certain distance. The amount of Kinetic Energy that the object has simply depends on its speed and its mass. We speak of an energetic person as one who is continually busy, in constant movement. Kinetic Energy, then, can be regarded as the capacity for doing work.

What made energy such a useful concept for scientists was the realisation that it could be converted into many different forms. The most important of these is Potential Energy, and the standard example of this is the energy that is stored in a compressed spring. or an elastic band. Imagine firing a ball from a catapult. You put the ball against the elastic band; you do work in pulling the band back, which is stored in the Potential Energy of the stretched elastic; you then release the band, and the Potential Energy gets converted into the Kinetic Energy of the moving ball. What made scientists in the nineteenth century so excited about energy was their realisation that they could work out in detail how mechanical systems behaved just by considering the ways in which energy was converted between different forms. Heat, for instance, is a form of energy: by using a steam engine the Heat Energy can be converted into the Kinetic Energy of motion.

In our everyday life we are continually concerned with energy although we do not usually refer to it as such. Many of us weigh ourselves, and displeased with what we see, we start counting calories. One food calorie (an example of chemical energy) is the energy released by a good-sized pinch of sugar when it is oxidised. To keep our human machine running efficiently we need a thousand or more calories of energy each day.

One of the householder's most commonly used form of energy is electricity. It is only when there is a cut in the supply that we become aware just how much we are dependent upon this commodity in daily life. Our freezer thaws, our heating goes off, no lights go on, we lose what we have been working on at our computer, we cannot boil water in our kettle even for a cup of tea, let alone cook anything for lunch. The doorbell does not work, and no radio, no TV. When we receive our electricity bill we will be charged for the number of kilowatt-hours we have used. If we have ten 100-watt light bulbs in our home they will require a kilowatt-hour between them every hour. We pay for electrical energy.

Energy in all its physical forms on Planet Earth can be traced back to our Sun, or to the stellar processes that gave birth to the Sun and the Earth. Each second in the core of the Sun the energy equivalent of four million tons changes from (potential) nuclear energy to light, Radiant Energy, which over the next few thousand years percolates outwards until it reaches the surface and illuminates us and the other planets.

Not all energy on Planet Earth is available to us, although with the present world energy crisis - fossil fuels running out and their burning detrimentally affecting our climate - we are seeking to tap other sources of energy: wind, waves, waterfalls, sunlight, etc.. The energy of the sea is vast but not yet available to us.

The fact that energy in its physical form can be measured, for instance, in kilowatt-hours, is at the heart of the physics of energy. Energy is conserved, meaning that when it is converted from one form into another, the total measured amount of energy remains the same.

Energy goes by so many names. Imagine I am holding a grenade in my hand. *Chemical Energy* describes its explosive power if I were to remove the pin and let go. While it is held in my hand it is gaining *Heat Energy*. Then comes the moment when I remove the pin and throw it - as far as possible! It travels through the air with *Kinetic Energy*, while *Gravitational Energy* causes it to fall towards the target. On hitting the ground it explodes and I see the flash - *Radiant Energy* - while the explosion deafens me with *Sound Energy*.

All these different forms of energy seem to make physics very complicated. But fortunately, in the twentieth century it was realised that by looking into the way matter is made up at the atomic level all these different sorts of energy could be explained in terms of the Kinetic Energy and Potential Energy of matter and fields. We will be looking at the idea of Fields in the next chapter, but a couple of examples will give the idea. When Heat Energy was discovered in the nineteenth century, it at first appeared very mysterious. But before long it was realised that it was nothing more than the Kinetic Energy of the atoms that made up any object, as they jostled together and bounced off each other.

A more subtle example is the idea of gravitational energy, which is a form of Potential Energy. In North Wales the Dinorwig power station uses gravitational energy to spread the demand for electricity more evenly. At times of low demand, such as during the night, electric energy from conventional gas-burning power stations is used in electric motors to power huge turbines that pump water uphill from the lake Llyn Peris to a reservoir Marchlyn Mawr. Then when more energy is needed during the day, the water is allowed to flow back through the same turbines, and the motors now act as generators to feed electric power back into the national grid. If energy is conserved, where does it go to while it is being used to pump the water uphill? If it is Potential Energy, where is the 'spring' that stores it? The solution came through the idea of the Gravitational Field, which is like a sort of universal, invisible springy material filling the whole universe. It is this that is 'wound up' as the water is pumped uphill, and this that acts as gravitational force that powers the turbines through the water as it flows back downhill.

But what is energy, and what is a field? We have seen what energy does, but what is its essence? With something as fundamental as this energy, this is a deep question, and we will need, in the next sections and the next chapter, to look more deeply even to find an inkling of an answer. In doing this we have to go beyond the ways we usually think. We like to think in terms of 'stuff'. Cars are made of steel, steel is made of iron and carbon, iron and carbon are made of various atomic particles ... but is there an ultimate "stuff" that everything is made of? Is energy the ultimate stuff, as some popular writers have suggested? Or is space-time itself the ultimate stuff, as Einstein came to believe in the latter part of his life, when he suggested that the material particle is nothing more than a highly concentrated and localised bundle of energy? Physicists now think that energy, in the physical sense that we have been using the word so far, must always be the energy *of* matter, or *of* a field, or *of* space-time. It is a property, not a stuff.

Energy and mass are different manifestations of the same property. If I weigh a stone, and then give energy to it by heating it up and weighing it again, it will be heavier, but only by a tiny amount, the relation between the two manifestations of this property being given by Einstein's famous formula $E=mc^2$, where E stands for energy and is equivalent to mass (m) multiplied by the square of the speed of light (c), But naming different forms gets us no nearer to its essence.

Most importantly, it is the principle of change, at such a basic level in physical theory that there is nothing more fundamental within present physics in terms of which it might be defined. We will see below how going beyond physics can enlarge the idea of energy to a principle that gives us an image of God, God manifest.

BEYOND PHYSICS

In this chapter I want to go beyond physics into metaphysics – into the area of thought and 'meaning' which is for us, as conscious beings, as much part of the world as the purely material, areas to which, in their subjective experienced quality, science has yet to extend itself. When we examine our own experience, we can see the way in which there is a principle of change that extends and enlarges the notion of energy.

Take the manifestation of energy as sound. Energy waves hit our eardrums, but it is the brain which interprets these waves as different sounds. Vibrations produce energy, which can be creative (causing resonance in octaves) or destructive (cracking wine glasses!). Why else does music have such a profound effect on us, whether it be Mozart or Heavy Metal? The concepts of creative and destructive take us beyond the quantitative realm of ordinary physics. There is another 'dimension' of energy here. Energy can be used constructively or destructively. If a dam is burst the Gravitational Energy released gives rise to destructive forces as, for example, the effect of the Dam-busters raid on Germany during World War II. If the water is released in a controlled fashion as at Dinorwig, the release of energy can be used to do useful work, to be creative, as in generating electricity in a hydroelectric scheme. Because these aspects that we perceive subjectively are beyond present physics, it does not necessarily mean that they are illusory.

We notice the increased interest today in what is sometimes called Subtle Energy, manifested in areas such as the placebo effect, intuition, angels, karma, synchronous channelling and other effects that belong to the area of consciousness.

These phenomena, which we experience in human life, have their principles of change, their dynamic of interchange of activity, which points to generalisations of the idea of energy. They are beyond the interest of scientists because they are beyond the physical realm. Some of them, like psychic energy, are manifested in ways that appear to be largely independent of space and time. Our mind activates electro-chemical impulses in the brain to produce thoughts. The thoughts express themselves as energy (which can be measured physically) and has an effect on the molecular structure of physical objects around us.

Experiments in the Institute of Somatic Science of Yunnan University in China have verified the existence of a 'thought field', which is independent of gravitational and electro-magnetic fields. The energy of this field interacts with the energy of matter. The existence of a thought field goes far in explaining many instances of the paranormal.

We recognise in this area the four major psychic phenomena, all of which seem to share a similar dynamic. One is Telepathy by which one person detects another's thoughts. There is Clairvoyance by which one becomes aware of events happening in another place. Precognition is the ability to predict an otherwise unpredictable future, while Psychokinesis is the affecting of physical processes just by willing them to change; bending spoons, for example. Traditionally these are considered to be 'gifts' possessed by the few, though the work of Dean Radin now indicates that they are present in a weak form in a large fraction of the population. In the East they are known as Sidhis: powers which transcend ordinary physical limits. These phenomena point to a wider view where these are all expressions of energy. And just as Gravitational Energy gave rise to the idea of a gravitational field to carry it, so these phenomena suggest a generalised sense of 'field'. At a higher level still we can speak of spiritual energy. The religions of the world are an immense reservoir of spiritual energy. All energy, I postulate, emanates from the Ultimate Reality we name God. So all energy has a divine dimension. It manifests the Divine Being

What is called energy by the scientist might be called spirit or grace by the priest. They are essentially the same. Their origin lies in the reality beyond our senses. Science cannot measure various human energies such as thought, desire, love, enthusiasm, hatred, anger, etc. all of which are emanations from the human psyche and motivators for action. While scientists may be able to detect brain activity related to these phenomena, they cannot actually measure their subjective essence , nor their true point of origin.

Science is unconcerned with the immaterial energies, or life energies, whose tremendous power has long been recognised by earlier cultures and individuals variously as Ch'i, Ka, Prana, Mana, Archeus, Vis Vitalis. Ch'i, for example is the life-force that moves along the energetic meridians of the body and which was pinpointed several thousand years ago by the Chinese and used for healing. An example of its use is well known to us: Acupuncture. The highest and most powerful form of energy experienced by human beings is unconditional Love. When John wrote (1 John 4) 'God is Love' he might equally have said - with the same truth but with far less appeal - 'God is the Love energy', the creating energy which sustains us. God is the sum of all energy relationships because God is the source of all energy, the Alpha and Omega of that energy which is Love.

GOD THE SOURCE OF CREATIVE ENERGY

The great energy of the Universe, the energy that will finally triumph is love. Teilhard de Chardin, the Jesuit mystic, palaeontologist, writes of 'the incredible power of love', 'the primal and universal psychic energy', 'the most universal, the most tremendous and the most mysterious of the cosmic forces' (*Human Energy*).

In physics, changes in energy can be either positive or negative. For example, the poles of a battery are termed positive and negative. But in the total picture of energy, these terms can be misleading. We can confuse the mathematical meaning of 'positive' with the spiritual meaning. Seen in this wider context, since all energy is a manifestation of God's creative energy, it can only be positive. In the world of human beings, however, negative effects of energy are experienced because human beings have the choice to misuse, abuse, over-use positive energy. We will say more about this in a later chapter.

There is sometimes confusion between energy and consciousness. Consciousness is the interior aspect of ourselves, the subjective feeling of our experience from moment to moment. At the physical level, energy is by contrast the exterior aspect of things. Every action (thought) of the brain generates a minuscule amount of physical energy. But in the more generalised sense of energy as the principle of change that I am suggesting here, the internal aspect of thought can also initiate events just as powerfully as the external aspect, by establishing a context of meaning and feeling, which enables things to change. So consciousness is associated with energy in the generalised sense of the principle of change. There is evidence that this aspect of consciousness extends beyond the individual. Many minds acting in coherence can produce a global effect, termed by parapsychologists as 'field effect', as has been demonstrated by the benefits it brings to the surroundings of people meditating together in large groups. This effect can be both beneficial and destructive. War generates a mass hatred of the perceived enemy.

While consciousness does not equal energy, yet the two are inseparable. Consciousness is the witness which experiences the flow of energy. Consciousness is our ability to feel, to know and to detect energy. God Manifest manifests as creative energy. God is the Supreme Consciousness, the source of the creative field of energy.

So we can say, that creative energy is God's free and undeserved gift to us. There is no other source of energy than Divine Energy. Since we owe our existence to this source it is a participation in the life of God. Think of creation as the continuous bursting forth of Divine Energy. The Big Bang was an explosion of energy: an explosion of Love given material form.

A helpful image of God can come from an analogy with the interplay of Potential Energy (the compressed spring or the compressed field) and the Kinetic Energy of motion. If we think of God Manifest as the Universe with all its workings and God Unmanifest as the intelligence, the consciousness, that is driving the workings of the manifest Universe, then God Unmanifest corresponds to Potential Energy and God Manifest to Kinetic Energy . Everything that goes on in the Universe is God made manifest by the conversion of God's unmanifest Potential Energy into manifest Kinetic Energy.

Just as we cannot see energy, so we cannot see God. We see, we experience, the effects of energy. We experience the effects of God. If such a way of conceiving that which is inconceivable, namely God, feels too impersonal, let us remember that we human beings reflect, as only human beings can, God's highest attributes, supreme consciousness and unconditional love, both of which are manifestations of energy.

3. THE FIELD

The Field is the only reality *(Einstein)*

In the previous chapter we met the idea of the gravitational field as a substance existing throughout all space that could store potential energy like a spring.

But we meet fields in many other ways. How can the airport security scanner discover metallic objects on you without touching you?   How is the MRI scanner, a device outside the body, able to take a detailed picture of your inside? These all happen through a different field: the electromagnetic field. As the name suggests, it combines electric and magnetic effects. It is the electric field that causes your wool vest to crackle as you pull it over your hair, and the magnetic field that causes a compass needle to point North, enabling us to find our bearings. This field, the first one to be considered by scientists, was introduced by the nineteenth century British scientist Michael Faraday (and like many great ideas was at first met with considerable scepticism).

So what is a 'field'? One can think of a field more generally as an area of influence. We speak of a person's field of influence: the extent of their power. Or of our field of vision meaning everything within range of our eyesight. The different kinds of field have different kinds of influence. The magnetic field influences magnets causing them to twist into a particular direction: a compass needle is a small magnet. The gravitational field causes all things on or near the surface of the Earth to be drawn towards the Earth. Fields influence things in particular ways, and they are themselves shaped and bent by different things in particular ways. So a magnet is influenced by the magnetic field, and a magnet itself shapes the magnetic field around it. You can make visible the shape of the magnetic field around a magnet by putting a piece of paper over it and sprinkling iron filings over the paper. Similarly, the Earth shapes the gravitational field around it so as to draw objects towards it. In cases like this, we say that the magnet of the Earth is the 'source' of the field (though strictly speaking they do not produce the field, but only shape it).

The extent to which a field is shaped by something decreases with distance. Every form of physical force or power has a limited range. Usually the closer the source, the greater the force or influence felt. Sometimes this influence can be very subtle. Biologists show us how various life forms such as birds and fish use the Earth's magnetic field to find their direction.

Some fields are much more forceful than others. The magnetic field, for instance, is far stronger than the gravitational field. Two magnets placed a few centimetres apart are attracted to each other with a force that is of roughly the same strength as the gravitational force that the entire body of the Earth exerts on them. What is striking about the gravitational field, however, is that it is so all-pervasive. We do not even stop to think about it, yet it influences every movement we make and all objects around us. It gives things weight and causes things to fall. The Moon moves around the Earth because of the Earth's shaping the gravitational field. The gravitational pull of the Moon causes the tides in our seas, while the gravitational influence of the Sun causes the Earth and the other planets to revolve around it.

THE WORLD OF FIELDS

Fields do not just passively receive shaping by objects, but they have a dynamic of their own. They can vibrate, just as a spring can, and so can transmit waves. In the case of the electro-magnetic field, of which the electric and magnetic fields are really just special forms, we detect these vibrations as different forms of rays. Some, such as light rays, we can see with our eyes. Most are not perceptible through our five senses. Some we can tune into with our radio and television sets. These fields enable objects to act upon one another even when they are not in material contact.

Unlike material objects, fields have a holistic quality. They are not diminished by being divided up. For instance, a magnet has two poles: one end attracts and the other repels, while the middle part is neutral. One can see these distinctions in the shape of the magnetic field. If one cuts the magnet in the middle one has two complete magnets, each with an attracting and a repelling pole, each adding its own complete structure to the magnetic field, in a holistic way.

It is the force of fields which causes everything in the Universe to relate to everything else and to have an effect on everything else. While many people today are in tune with this new vision of the unity underlying all reality - even if they have not heard about the scientific Field Theory - the fact remains, however, that all our major institutions, be they political, social, ecclesiastical, economic, still operate as if everything existed independently of the separate parts comprising it. Many of the major issues affecting our lives, and the lives of those who make and implement major decisions, are largely untouched by this new vision. They are still immersed in the old 'mechanical' consciousness. They still attempt to dominate, manipulate and control the world by controlling different sections and parts in isolation from the others.

The picture presented by the theory of fields is quite different. Imagine a number of corks floating in a basin of water. If we touch one and make it bob, waves of water travel outwards and make all the others bob too. The solar system moves through the gravitational field. Human society is sometimes described as a field. In all these cases, when one part changes, the whole is affected almost simultaneously, because all parts are intimately connected. Einstein spoke of a field as: 'A totality of existing facts, which are conceived of as mutually dependent'.

The introduction of the concept of fields, and their progressive unification, were huge steps that revealed a Universe far more connected and unified than Newton would have imagined. But there are several more, equally huge steps before we reach what many writers refer to as 'The Field'.

In the picture of the corks bobbing about on water, the corks are clearly distinct from the water. The corks are distinct and separate, the water is continuous and unifying. This was the picture at the start of the twentieth century, where matter was made up of distinct and separate atoms, while fields introduced unity. It was a sort of half-way house en route to the modern picture. The next step came with quantum theory, when it was realised that matter itself is more like a field than like particles. Here is not the place to go into the intricacies of quantum theory, but something of the flavour of it is expressed by a phrase of the influential philosopher of quantum theory, Bernard d'Espagnat, who refers to 'veiled reality'. It seems that behind the appearances of laboratory physics there is a domain which physicists can only describe through abstract mathematical formalism. This quantum domain is real, because its properties can be rigorously tested by calculation and experiment on laboratory phenomena; but it is veiled because we have no direct access to it. One symptom of its veiling is the fact that it can be described by many different mathematical structures, all equally good – which is why studying quantum theory is so confusing! Importantly, however, all the structures suggested for the quantum domain deal with fields or field-like things. I am going to use the phrase 'quantum fields' for these structures, although physicists use this term in a more restricted sense.

So behind the world of our senses, of distinct solid objects, there is a world of quantum fields. Some of these are quantum versions of the fields we have just been looking at, the electromagnetic and gravitational fields, which are called 'classical fields' (that is, non-quantum fields). Others are purely quantum fields which give rise to matter, and which can manifest as particles called electrons, protons, neutrons and so on. Though they are called particles, these have ambiguous properties, sometimes looking like particles in the way that we speak of grains of sand as particles; but sometimes being spread out over space and looking like classical fields. Behind all this, however, is a deeper, but veiled, world of pure fields.

The main focus in fundamental physics over the last forty years or so has been understanding this world. It has led to an increasingly unified understanding of the way in which all these fields fit together. I have already mentioned how the magnetic and the electric field can act together as the electromagnetic field, which has new properties: it can vibrate and produce rays. It is this combination that enables electric motors to work - in fact, it would be impossible really to understand electric and magnetic fields separately, they are so closely linked. It was only when scientists like Faraday realised this that the laws governing electricity and magnetism could be unravelled. So the question arose, could this process of combining fields be repeated with other fields in nature? Might we get more and more understanding of what fields really are by combining them yet further? The answer seems to be, yes. There are other fields responsible for nuclear reactions, taking place in the very heart of atoms and acting with a very short range. Their corresponding influences are unimaginatively called 'The Weak Force' and 'The Strong Force'. The Weak Force governs certain forms of radioactive decay. It contributes to heating the radioactive rock deep within the Earth's interior which drives the volcanoes. The Strong Force provides the energy that fuels the stars and creates the life-giving rays of the Sun. Between 1961 and 1967 the physicists Salam, Glashow and Weinberg discovered that the weak field could be combined with the electromagnetic field in what is now called the 'electro-weak field'. At the same time, the quantum fields describing different particles of matter were integrated into this picture. This made everything even more under-standable: one could understand why each of the separate fields had to have its own particular behaviour, and a host of new phenomena became understandable.

The next step has been the incorporation of the Strong Field, a project whose outline is now fairly well understood. The result is called the Grand Unified Theory (or GUT). Only one more field remains to be integrated: the gravitational field. Achieving this is the Holy Grail of physicists. A current attempt is known as the M theory. Understand this and they might be able to formulate a 'Theory of Everything' (TOE); a complete description of all the forces of the Universe and their interaction. John Barrow, in his book *Theories of Everything: the Quest for the Ultimate Explanation*, believes that there is a graspable logic behind the physical existence that can be compressed into one formula. And the concluding sentence of Stephen Hawking's famous book *A Brief History of Time* reads:

> If we do discover a complete theory, it should in time be understandable in broad principle by everyone, not just a few scientists. Then we shall all, philosophers, scientists and just ordinary people, be able to take part in the discussion of why it is that we and the Universe exist. If we find the answer to that, it would be the ultimate triumph of human reason - for then we would truly know the mind of God.

To know the mind of God is to know God Manifest. For God Manifest is the energising Spirit of the Universe. It is the life force flowing through the

Universe, called by theologians the Holy Spirit.

The world of fields is a vast network of ultimate energy, the principle of change at the physical level. Considered as energy, it manifests itself as 'dark energy': a gravitational influence throughout the Universe, discovered over the last 10 years, whose effect is to cause the expansion of the Universe to accelerate continually. 73% of the measurable energy of the Universe is made up of Dark Energy, and 23% of Dark Matter, probably the quantum fields of forms of matter predicted by GUT but not yet discovered in the laboratory. What we know of ordinary matter (the stars, etc) makes up only 4%.

FROM FIELDS TO `THE FIELD'

But let's leave the physicists to their search, for theirs is only one aspect, the physical aspect, of the world. Their expertise is physical energy; energy that can be measured. Beyond this, however, are phenomena such as those called `paranormal' (telepathy and clairvoyance) which have now been conclusively shown to exist through repeatable experiments. Premonition is another example. How often have we felt an urge to telephone a friend we have not contacted for some time, to have our call met with: 'How funny, I was just going to call you'. These happenings seem to have properties reminiscent of quantum fields, but they stubbornly refuse to be fitted within scientific theories as they have so far developed. This has led the experimentalist Dean Radin to suggests that a quite new way of thinking is needed in order to extend the world of fields so as to understand these phenomena. What we need to explore are the metaphysical aspects of the world of fields, which are beyond the scientist's remit

THE REALM OF SPIRIT - the Metaphysical - the Paranormal
The state of transcendence - The unified field of
consciousness

> No mass
> No space-time
> The eternal NOW. timeless
> Formless
> Immeasurable
> Unknowable to our five senses
> Realm of intuition, of mysticism

above

=================================*speed of light*

below

THE PHYSICAL UNIVERSE - the normal

> Positive energy
> Positive mass
> Positive space-time
> Gravity bound
> Having form
> Measurable
> Knowable to the senses
> Realm of the intellect

– the realm of spirit. (See diagram.) We are familiar with the physical world, our everyday world – this is evident to our senses – and scientists have added to this the mathematical quantum world, but most people are less aware that we also live in the metaphysical realm in which we can experience the paranormal, experiences which are not measurable. When a person's consciousness transcends in deep meditation, the mind of that meditator enters the realm of spirit.

Those who study the effects of group meditation speak of meditators having a subjective experience of the Unified Field of Pure Consciousness. They claim that the pure consciousness experience in meditation is actually a direct experience by the human nervous system of a Field that goes beyond the physical. But this is more than an individual experience. Although we tend to think of individuals affecting one another only through some form of social contact, research by Radin and others has shown that human consciousness acts more like the quantum field – more like the bobbing corks - than balls on a billiard table touching each other one at a time. The fields produced by the nervous system of each individual person appear to be able to merge. Each is an aspect of the same field of consciousness. So we speak of a 'field of collective consciousness'. It is in this sense that I shall speak of 'The Field' in the following sections.

ANIMALS RELATE THROUGH THE FIELD

We experience the effect at the human level but there are many instances in the animal world of communication by means of The Field. A flock of birds will take off at the same moment and all change direction in their flight simultaneously. A shoal of fish change direction in the water instantaneously as if one body. Whales can communicate with each other over vast distances. Is this by sound or by thought transfer? Dolphins appear to have a quite extraordinary ability to communicate with the human mind. Colonies of ants and bees may co-ordinate their activities with the help of telepathy. Rupert Sheldrake has experimented with people staring at other people with their backs to them and noting how often the latter become aware of being stared at. In his book *Dogs that Know when their Owners are coming Home* he gives many instances of the telepathic communication between humans and their dogs, cats and horses. It is noteworthy that very few wild animals were killed in the tsunami floods in Asia on Boxing Day 2004. They sensed it was coming and went up onto higher ground. We are still studying how it is that swallows, with their tiny brains, are able to migrate 6,000 miles between South Africa and England to the same places each year, even to the same nest in which they were born. Are they sensitive to the Earth's magnetic fields, or to the deeper aspects of The Field? We, sophisticated human beings appear to have lost our ability to be perceptive, to communicate telepathically, as our early ancestors could. Yet we still find the exception, as when for example, someone suddenly feels physical pain when their twin, hundreds of miles away, is the victim of a road accident. Guy Playfair, in his book *Twin Telepathy*, claims that about 30% of twins experience telepathic intercommunication. Another instance is when The Field is misused, as when a witch sticks pins in a doll with the purpose of causing harm to a distant person.

In his book *A New Science of Life* (first published in 1983) Rupert Sheldrake proposes his theory of

Morphogenic Fields, a theory he has been developing with various practical experiments in the years following. We will be seeing in later chapters how this relates to many of our Christian beliefs. He defines Morphic Fields as: 'Non-material regions of influence extending in space and continuing in time'. Another definition is: The influence of like upon like through space and time. A classic example, noted in the 1920s when milk was delivered to houses in bottles with cardboard caps, was that of blue tits learning to tear off the caps of milk bottles to obtain the cream. Within a short space of time, blue tits elsewhere, well beyond the range of normal communication, had learnt the same trick. There are instances of someone making a scientific breakthrough, in say, the USA., while the same discovery is made by a scientist in Russia or Japan, with no normal communication having been made between them. Charles Darwin is well known for his theory of evolution published in his 1859 book *The Origin of Species*. Less well-known is the name of a Welshman, Alfred Russell Wallace, who in his work in the Amazon Basin and later in the Malay Archipelago had come up with the same theory of evolution by natural selection. In fact, it was his sending his memoir to Darwin from Moluccas in 1858 that prompted Darwin to publish his own findings the following year. The two had worked quite independently. Can we detect telepathy again here?

The Jesuit mystic, palaeontologist, Teilhard de Chardin, speaks of The Field as the Noosphere, an expression he picked up from the Russian Professor Vladimir Vernadski who lived at the beginning of the 19th century in Moscow. He conceived of it as being a sphere or crystallisation of human spiritual energy.

Teilhard describes it as: 'The thinking envelope of the Earth'. According to him it comprises:

- the growth of a collective memory
- the development of a generalised nervous system covering the entire surface of the globe
- the growth of a faculty of common vision
- a planetary arrangement of human mass and energy.

The conflict that we are experiencing between the wealth and power of the western world and the poverty and suffering of the southern hemisphere is caused by the massive energy imbalance in the body of The Field around our planet.

OUR COMMON CONSCIOUSNESS

In *The Future of Man* Teilhard speaks of the Noosphere as: 'The rise on our inward horizon of a cosmic spiritual centre, a supreme pole of consciousness, upon which all the separate consciousnesses of the world may converge and within which they may love one another.' His view is shared by a number of scientists today (Konstantin Korotkov, Karl Pribram, Gary Schwartz, Hal Puthoff, David Hawkins among them) who regard the human brain as a transducer, retrieving, reading out and transmitting information, similar to the function of a radio. David Hawkins writes: 'The individual human mind is like a computer terminal connected to a giant database. The database is human consciousness itself, of which our own consciousness is merely an individual expression, but with its roots in the common consciousness of all mankind' (*Power vs Force*). And I would add: the

common consciousness of all humankind is a participation in the divine creative consciousness.

Amit Goswami writes (*The Physics of the Soul*):

> You and I have individual thoughts, feelings,
> dreams, etc, but we don't have consciousness, let
> alone separate ones; we are consciousness. And it is
> the same consciousness for all of us ...
> Consciousness is the ground of being; we cannot
> turn it off.

That there is only one consciousness in which we all
participate offers an explanation for the variety of
psychological and paranormal phenomena which are
unexplained by the traditional Newtonian understanding of the Universe.

On account of our interconnectedness through our
common consciousness, every thought we have, every
choice we make, every act we perform every moment
of the day must affect every other person in the world
– for good or for bad – and beyond time, affecting the
living, the dead and the yet-to-be born.

Consciousness is at the centre of all change. Divine
consciousness creates the Universe. As the quantum
field brings about material reality – causing an electron
(a particle) to materialise from the electron quantum
field – so, if we see the quantum field as an aspect of
the universal consciousness of The Field, we can
understand how petitionary prayer, by which we bring
our desires to the surface of our consciousness with the
power of intention, can cause our desire to materialise.

Perhaps the best summary of this vast subject is
offered by David Lorimer in his book *Whole in One*:

1. There is one Field of Consciousness in which we live and move and have our being.

2. Within this Field we are holons (relatively autonomous subtotalities), or thinking, feeling and willing beings.

3. Although we are inseparable from The Field, which constitutes our underlying identity as revealed in unitive consciousness, we are nevertheless distinct in form and may have the sensory illusion that we are in fact quite independent.

4. We act on and in The Field in such a way that the results of our thinking, feeling and willing return to us in a dynamic feedback loop.

5. In the interconnectedness and interdependence within The Field are the ultimate context of our moral responsibility. The Field is not mocked.

6. The dynamics of The Field are such that they elicit Love, which is its essential nature. The feedback of loving thoughts and actions is love and joy, while hatred and bitterness breed isolation and sorrow. Each feedback constitutes a lesson in learning the art of loving and realising the inescapability of our interconnectedness as illustrated in the reciprocity of the Golden Rule.

Wherever we stand with our feet on Planet Earth we are all separate expressions of consciousness, while one with the Supreme Consciousness. When we leave Earth through death we continue as expressions of consciousness, but then become fully aware of our oneness with the Supreme Consciousness.

We shall be seeing in a later chapter that the core of the Good News of Jesus from Nazareth is that we are born to experience this unity with the Divine: that God lives in us and we in God. In the course of our physical evolution, without any deliberate act on our part, we became self-conscious – described in the mythical language of The Fall – and perceived ourselves as separate from God as from all else and all other creatures. The invitation of Jesus is to move on to a further stage: purposefully to identify our consciousness with the consciousness of God. This is our eternal destiny. Maybe heaven is the biblical name for realms of higher energy, of supreme consciousness, existing beyond the limitations of the material.

4. GOD IN NATURE

A mistake in one's understanding of Creation will necessarily cause a mistake in one's understanding of God.
(St Thomas Aquinas)

The memory will always remain with me of a chapel I once visited in the north of England. The whole of the east wall, behind the altar, was made of glass, so as one prayed in front of the altar one was able to look beyond at a wonderful scene of fields and woods and hills in the distance. I was able to experience the presence of God in two dimensions, as it were: at the centre of our liturgy at the altar and present in nature beyond.

In both the Hebrew Scriptures (the Christian Old Testament) and in the New Testament we find mention of the way in which God can be known through nature. The Church calls this Natural Revelation.

So we read in the Book of Wisdom (13:1): 'Naturally stupid are all who have not known God and who, from the good things that are seen, have not been able to discover Him-who-is, or by studying the works, have failed to recognise the Artificer.' And the apostle Paul wrote (Romans 1:20): 'Ever since God created the world, His invisible qualities, both His eternal power and His divine nature, have been clearly seen: they are perceived in the things that God has made.' When Paul and Barnabas were preaching the Good News in Lystra, Paul cured a crippled man. The crowd immediately jumped to the conclusion that Paul and Barnabas must be gods: 'The gods have become like men and have come down to us!' They gave Barnabas the name Zeus and Paul the name Hermes. They brought bulls and flowers and wanted to offer sacrifice to the apostles. In assuring them of their error the apostles said: '[God] has always given evidence of His existence by the good things He does: He gives you rain from heaven and crops at the right times; He gives you food and fills your hearts with happiness' (Acts 14:8-17). However, God is not self-evident in the Universe but is known only through a faith response to experience.

A contemporary theologian and cultural historian, Thomas Berry, says in *The Dream of the Earth*: 'The Universe itself, but especially the planet Earth, needs to be experienced as the primary mode of divine presence'. And elsewhere he calls the created Universe 'the primary religious reality, the primary revelation of the Divine'.

The late Donald Nicholl, one-time rector of Tantur Ecumenical Centre in Jerusalem, wrote in *The Tablet* (2/4/88):

I believe that many of the discussions and controversies on religious issues these days are frustrating and paralyse our capacity for spiritual growth because most of us are operating with a world view at the back of our minds which is the world view of late nineteenth century scientific materialism ... a world view that made the Universe seem hostile to us and thereby made us feel ourselves to be excrescences upon it, aliens in the Universe.

Do we not speak of 'conquering nature' as if it were a force quite apart from us humans?

I believe there are three areas of life today that are causing us to re-adjust our relationship to our planet: to 'operate' with an up-to-date world view.

RE-ADJUSTING OUR RELATIONSHIP TO OUR PLANET

The first is caused by the increasing number of reports and warnings that we are receiving about global warming and of the alarming consequences to the whole planet, not to mention the effect it will have on the everyday lives of millions of people – mostly the poorest people – unless we take the matter seriously and each of us makes some contribution within our small circle to conserve energy. Disastrously, a lot of people are taking little notice of the alarm bells ringing because this is such a turn-around of attitude held by the western world over the last centuries, certainly since the Industrial Revolution.

Past generations have been brought up on an understanding of the passages of Genesis about our place on Earth as meaning that we could *use* nature in any way we wished to supply for our needs. This interpretation of such passages as: 'Then God said: "And now we will make human beings; they will be like us and resemble us. They will have *power* over the fish, the birds and all animals, domestic and wild, large and small"' (1:26). And in verse 28 God is saying 'Be fruitful, multiply, fill the Earth and *conquer* it'. And in Psalm 8 we read:' You appointed him [man] over everything you made: you placed him over all creation'. This sense of our being apart from, above, outside the rest of creation (because we regarded ourselves alone as made in the image of God) has persisted throughout the history of Christianity. It was held together with the belief that our prime purpose in life was to *use* nature as a means to reach Heaven, because getting to Heaven was what life was all about. Nature could be dominated, exploited, ravaged as a means to that end. We find this idea expressed by the great theologian of the Middle Ages, St Thomas Aquinas. Anxious to move away from the earlier Gnostic negative view of the world and of the human body, he taught that the world is not just neutral but good. However, it is good, not on its own account, but only because it serves our human needs.

We find the same view expressed in one of the most influential writings on western spirituality, originating in the 16th century but claiming increasing popularity today: the *Spiritual Exercises of St Ignatius*. There we read:

> Man has been created to praise, reverence and serve our Lord God, thereby saving his soul. Everything on Earth has been created for man's sake, to help him achieve the purpose for which he has been created.

A NEW UNDERSTANDING OF ECOLOGY

Secondly, our present climatic situation is shifting our consciousness to a new understanding of ecology. Concerned though we are, or are becoming, about preserving our environment, our present attitude is human-centred. Regarding our world as apart from ourselves; we are above and outside the rest of nature.

What we are doing environmentally we are doing for our own preservation rather than that of the whole of creation. We are valuing everything according to how it relates to us: we regard its use value. It is this same attitude which creates hierarchical structures: judging some things, some people, more important than others. It is their use that gives them importance. Setting some things, some people, above others has resulted in patriarchy, in racialism (other races are inferior to ours), in imperialism (we of the West have so much to give the less endowed people of the Third World), and from that follows exploitation. Another manifestation of this is religious superiority: my God is the true God. There can be no dialogue with people holding that view.

The Norwegian philosopher Arne Naess refers to the above attitude as 'shallow ecology' and compares it with what he calls 'deep ecology'. By this he means appreciating that humanity is part of the natural environment. We human beings are not superior to any other creature on the planet, because all living beings have, not a worth value, but an intrinsic value, whether it be a tree, the cat next door or you or me. Everything in nature is fundamentally interconnected and interdependent. We all belong together. We all need each other. Surely the basis of this attitude is the appreciation that everything, but everything, is a reflection of the Divine, everything is empowered by the divine creative energy. This is a panentheistic view. We are actually reclaiming an awareness that our ancestors had and which we can still find in the appreciation of nature by the Aborigines, the North American Indians and in the Celtic culture. We in the western world have made tremendous technological advances, using all the natural resources available, but our regarding the Earth as spiritual has not kept pace. We simply regard it as a resource. We urgently need a spiritual revolution to accompany our technological revolution. It should be added that the appreciation that Jesus had of creation can be seen in how he valued people. Valuing people, not for their worth to society, but as reflections of the Divine was why he embraced everyone equally: children, women, lepers, tax collectors, public sinners, the possessed. He considered no one person as superior to another.

> The Pharisees went off and made a plan to trap Jesus with questions. Then they sent to him some of their disciples and some members of Herod's party. 'Teacher,' they said, 'we know that you tell the truth about God's will for man, without worrying about what people think, because you pay no attention to a man's status'. (Matthew 22:15-16)

OUR PLACE IN SPACE

The third area causing us to re-adjust our thinking of who we are in relation to all of creation – one might say from the centre, as in pre-Galileo times, to the periphery – is due to the discoveries made by astro-physicists. Space, as we call it, is so vast that distances can only be measured in light-years, the time it takes for light to travel between, for example, ourselves and the stars when light travels at a speed on 186,000 miles per second; the fastest physical speed we are able to measure. A light year is shorthand for 5.880,000,000,000 miles! Just as a 'plane travelling at supersonic speed leaves its sound wave behind it, so if we were to travel faster than light the electromagnetic fields which hold our atoms together would be left behind us and we would disintegrate.

Our Earth is just one planet in our Solar System, and the nearest star to us (after the Sun which is only 92,955,800 miles away) is *Proxima Centauri* which is four light years away. Our Milky Way galaxy, consisting of some 100 billion stars, measures 100,000 light years across and it is only one of a cluster of galaxies, each cluster being part of a super cluster of many thousands of galaxies. This is all within the scope of the tiny part we know! What is beyond?

Far from thinking of ourselves as the final and most perfect product of the Creator's hand, we now have to see ourselves as mere dots on a vast canvas. We all live on one tiny planet. How can we be so pompous as to think we human beings are so special!

Incidentally, we have to understand when we read the Bible, that the cosmology of people two thousand and more years ago was extremely limited. They knew no more about space than they could see: the blue sky was the roof of the Universe with its stars and sun and moon. And their God was just up there, above the clouds, ever so near to them, so no wonder they felt so special. When the gospel writers spoke of the risen Jesus departing from their presence they spoke of him 'ascending' to Heaven, a cloud conveniently hiding him from further view. The sky God was immediately involved with their everyday events. Yet isn't this the manner in which so many people still today regard their relationship with God? And isn't this the reason why so many others, more aware of today's cosmology, rightly reject that image of God?

PARTNERS WITH GOD

In an earlier book (*The Creative Christian*) I wrote of the way in which we human beings are invited to partner God in the process of evolution. We are not of course equal partners because the initiative comes from God as does the creative energy which enables our participation. For God, being in the perpetual NOW, the Universe has reached its final end. But for us living in created time-space it has still to be worked out in our future.

This poses the question: if, in the mind of God, all exists in the NOW moment of eternity – where time is non-existent – how are we to partner God, bringing Him down, so to speak, into our time-bound world? Arthur Peacocke, priest and scientist, gives us a useful musical analogy in an essay *Articulating God's Presence in and to the World Unveiled by the Sciences:*

> When we are listening to a musical work, say, a Beethoven piano sonata, there are times when we are so deeply absorbed in it that for the moment we are thinking Beethoven's musical thoughts with him. Yet if anyone were to ask at that moment (unseemly interrupting our concentration!), 'Where is Beethoven now?' we could only reply that Beethoven-as-composer is to be found only in the music itself. Beethoven-as-composer was or is – for this could have been said even when he was alive – other than the music (he 'transcends' it), but his communication with us is entirely subsumed in and represented by the music itself: he is immanent in it and we need not look elsewhere to meet him in that creating role.

We have always told ourselves that we are 'made in the image of God'. But God is a creating God so we too are creating beings. We have been gifted with imagination, with a desire to better ourselves and the conditions of life around us, to seek new and better ways of doing things, above all to look for ways of overcoming the pains and sufferings that humanity endures. When new advances are made in science – particularly in those branches which affect human beings' personal lives – the warning sounds: 'Beware! We are playing God'. It is a warning that we are overstepping the boundary line that is supposed to exist between what human beings are permitted (by God presumably) to achieve through our own efforts and increased knowledge and what is the domain of God. But who draws this line? Who, if not God, is to decide what is human business and what is God's business? And if it is God who decides the boundary, how are we to know where it lies?

Whatever further steps we take to promote our future evolution – wresting such powers from God, so to speak – we can be certain that they must have been written into the structure of the Universe as God originally willed it, but only now are their potentialities being realised.

PLAYING GOD

To play God in the sense of utilising our God-given intelligence in order to benefit increasingly from the potential of the created world is our human destiny. But hidden in that ability is the danger of playing God in the sense of obtaining more and more control over nature for our own selfish purposes, such that a minority of people gain control over the lives of the majority.

In our human history there have been several clear leaps across a supposed God-human dividing line: leaps which enabled our ancestors to achieve what their forebears would hardly have dared dream of. The first, the greatest as far as our human evolution was concerned, was the leap out of the mythical Garden of Eden: the leap from undifferentiated union towards differentiated union because we had become self-aware, aware of our identity as individuals. The next must have been the ability to make fire. Then, thousands of years later, what the German philosopher, Karl Jaspers, has called the Axial Age (approx. 600-300 BCE) when a great leap of consciousness was made in four distinct regions of the world and the great religious traditions, that are still with us today, were born: Confucianism and Daoism in China, Hinduism and Buddhism in India, monotheism in Israel through the great prophets and philosophical rationalism in Greece through Pythagoras, Socrates, Plato and Aristotle. (Writers regard today's evolution of consciousness as a comparable leap, calling it the Second Axial Age.) The next great take-over of divine power must have been with the Industrial Revolution with all its consequences. With this, humanity felt itself to be more self-sufficient; less needing than previously to call upon divine intervention to achieve mechanical wonders.

I would mark August 6th 1945 as a date when we crossed further into God's domain. By exploding the first atomic bomb over Hiroshima, killing 75,000 people and injuring tens of thousands more, we moved from an ability to commit mass homicide to the capability of omnicide. From that moment we seized from God control of our planet. From now on it is we, not God, who decide whether to maintain it in its evolutionary course or whether to destroy it all with one mighty explosion.

And today we are taking further steps to cross over God's boundary with our experiments in genetic engineering.

Each threshold crossed faces us with new moral problems for which there are no given guidelines. We have to make our own decisions with as broad a perspective as we are able. Are we 'playing God'? Yes, why not, if we are made in the image of a perpetually creating God?

5. THE CREATIVE ENERGY

God makes things make themselves
(Adapted from Mother Carey in *The Water Babies* by
Charles Kingsley)

The word 'creation' can cover a variety of meanings. In everyday speech it means to produce something new. I have never sat in front of a catwalk to watch the display of the latest fashions, but I do know they are referred to as creations. In this sense, creation presumes starting from ingredients or materials that already exist.

The word is used in a theological context to mean that God made the universe 'out of nothing'. But here our imagination plays tricks. It is hard not to picture God starting with a lump of 'nothing'! Theologians use the phrase *ex nihilo* but they do not mean 'out of nothing'. They mean 'from no thing'.

The problem our imagination has arises from our concept of time. We loosely speak of what there might have been before creation. But there was no before. Both time and space are the outcome of creation. Since time and space are interconnected – you cannot have one without the other – and since the Big Bang marked the coming into existence of space, it must also mark the coming into existence of time. There was no time before the Big Bang: there was no *before*. It follows that there could have been no pre-existent cause of the Big

Bang. This understanding of time-space by quantum physics lays to rest the popular notion of God first existing alone and then (in time) deciding to create the Universe.

CAUSE AND EFFECT

Traditionally, God is held to be the first cause or Creator of the Universe. In fact the need for a first cause - on the presumption that every effect has a cause - was one of the proofs for the existence of God offered by that theological colossus of the Middle Ages, St Thomas Aquinas. Today, scientists are abandoning Aristotelian metaphysics with its complex theories of causation. The need for a cause at the sub-atomic level has now been disproved. Things happen without being caused. Besides, the cause-effect relationship presumes the existence of time - one thing following another - and as we have seen, there was no time before creation.

This does not dispense with a creator God, only with our image of Him. While scientists are discovering this scenario in our own time, St Augustine arrived at the same conclusion fifteen hundred years earlier, without any knowledge of the Big Bang or four-dimensional space-time! He wrote in his *Confessions*:

It is idle to look for time before creation, as if time can be found before time. If there were no motion of either a spiritual or corporeal creature by which the future, moving through the present, would succeed the past, there would be no time at all .... We should therefore say that time began with creation, rather than that creation began with time.

It makes no sense to think of God pre-dating the Universe. This is not to say that I am following the line of Stephen Hawking who asks in his best-selling *A Brief History of Time*: 'What place then for a creator?'

Confusion occurs because of the very word *creation*. I would make a plea that we distinguish 'creation' from 'origin'. Scientists use 'creation' to mean the origin. What has been said above is about the origin of the Universe, how it all began. I prefer to use the word 'creation' for the ongoing cause of existence in the present moment: all reality held in existence by the Ultimate Reality, God. Indeed, all reality is but an expression, a materialisation in time-space of Ultimate Reality. Creation, in this sense, is the present-moment manifestation of divine energy, the under-girding energy of creation. God uses created time to relate to the Universe.

THE CREATIONIST'S VIEW

I am discounting the interpretation of our origins as given in the first chapters of the Book of Genesis, and upheld literally by some creationists even today. There still exists a small handful of Christians who believe God created the world on the 23rd of October 4004 BCE. This calculation was made in the early 1600s by James Ussher, Archbishop of Armagh. (It was improved upon by the Vice-Chancellor of Cambridge University, Dr Lightfoot, who claimed, in 1642 that creation actually took place at 9.00 am on that date!) It is now generally accepted, that our Universe came into existence some fourteen billion years ago with an explosion named by the scientist Sir Fred Hoyle, the 'Big Bang'. More recently the adjective 'big' is being questioned since one theory gaining ground today is that our Universe is not the only Universe. There is also a meta-universe (or Metaverse as it is sometimes called) existing prior to the Big Bang which produced our particular Universe. (Others speak of a Multiverse, meaning that there could be several Universes existing simultaneously.)

Did the authors of the first chapters of Genesis know something we don't know? They did not write that God created from nothing, they wrote: ' The Earth [today read 'the Universe'] was a formless void, there was darkness over the deep, and God's Spirit hovered over the water' (verse 2). In other words, God created order out of chaos. (The first biblical mention of creation *ex nihilo* is in 2 Maccabees: 'Observe heaven and earth, consider all that is in them, and acknowledge that God made them out of what did not exist' (7:28).)

So the Big Bang is not necessarily the beginning of time. Almost all ancient civilizations held that time is cyclic. Some still do. The Metaverse is the mother of our Universe and perhaps of myriad other universes. Nor will it cease to exist when our particular Universe vanishes in the collapse of a Black Hole.

However, our concern here is not with a God 'out there', 'before' there was a Universe, but with God as the sustainer of creation, empowering it from within. God is not an existent object: God is the source of all existence. As the source of existence, God's presence can be discovered in the world, which is not to say God is identified with the world (pantheism).

HAS CREATION A PURPOSE?

This raises the question for Christian theologians as to whether there is a purpose behind creation. Is it going somewhere? Does our Universe have a purpose? Accepting that it is evolving, what is it evolving towards? Nobody can know with the certainty of scientific fact.

We have to acknowledge that while there is growth there is also deterioration. Disease and death are as intrinsic to evolution as is life. Pain is essential to biological life as causing an awareness that something is wrong. The more complex the nervous system, the greater the pain felt. Death is a normal and inevitable aspect of biological life. 90% of species are already extinct. Or put another way, fewer than 10% of all species that ever swam, crawled or flew are still on Earth today. Biologists speak of our now bringing about the 6th major extinction of species. It is reckoned that 50% of species currently alive will have disappeared by the end of this century.

Theologians speculate on an answer to evolution's future in the light of Christian revelation. We read: 'In all his wisdom and insight God did what he had purposed, and made known to us the secret plan he had already decided to complete by means of the Christ. This plan, which God will complete when the time is right, is to bring all creation together, everything in the heavens and on earth, with Christ as head.' (Ephesians 1:9-10). Since the monotheistic religions of the West always make the distinction between the Creator and creation our ultimate destiny is spoken of as being united *with* God, with the divine consciousness. This differs from the eastern religions which speak of our ultimate destiny as being absorbed *into* the Godhead, into divine consciousness. But these are just human ways of speculating about the unknown. The ultimate experience will be beyond human description.

We are creatures. We have no other place except within creation. We are part of this Universe. Even when we die we will remain within creation, possibly existing on a different plane, in a different wavelength.

The fact is that nobody, but nobody, knows what state we will be in after we die because no one has ever come back to tell us. What we believe our destiny is, is a matter of faith, not fact. Each religion has its answer to that mystery. We can, however, get a clue from the many near-death experiences that are being recounted today.

But let us stay with the reality of the present. One thing we do know is that everything around us has evolved from less complex states. Whereas philosophers will maintain that the cause of something must be greater than the effect, in evolutionary terms it is a prerequisite that the potential for a higher state must be present in a lower state, from the start. The acorn contains the potential to become an oak tree.

THREE UNDERSTANDINGS OF THE CREATION PROCESS

There are three ways in which evolution has been understood. Scientists, such as Richard Dawkins, regard the process simply as a scientific fact with a scientific cause. Then there is the Darwinian theory which is concerned with the *how* of evolution rather than the original cause. And thirdly, there is a spiritual understanding, such as that of Teilhard de Chardin seeing the process as the unfolding of God's plan for leading creation to a point of unity, the Omega point, as he named it. He wrote of:

> The rise on our inward horizon of a cosmic spiritual centre, a supreme pole of consciousness, upon which all the separate consciousnesses of the world may converge and within which they may love one another: the *rise of a God*.

We know that evolutionary transformation takes place at an ever-increasing speed. If the fourteen billion years of our planet's evolution is diagrammatically posited on the 24 hours of one day, then we human beings arrived only a few minutes before midnight and our computer age began half a second ago. Although human beings appeared so recently in evolutionary terms, how little we know about our origins.

Among the different hypotheses is one that the descent of different races of humanity is from different original ancestors: Polygenism. This hypothesis challenges traditional Christian belief in the nature and transmission of Original Sin.

It must be said that the hypothesis of polygenism is not widely held. It came into mainstream scientific thought due to the work of Samuel George Morton and more prominently by Louis Agassiz in the United States. The issue of race was polemical, and slave owners attempted to justify their treatment of slaves using empirical science. They argued that each race was a different species and that black Africans were mentally inferior to Caucasians.

In the late 20th-century, the work of the paleoanthropologist Carleton Coon was the closest to what can perhaps be considered a 'modern' polygenism by suggesting that the individual races of the Earth separately evolved into modern *Homo sapiens*. This hypothesis is called the multiregional hypothesis.

The multiregional hypothesis holds that some or all of the genetic variations between contemporary human races are attributable to genetic inheritance from hominid species that were geographically dispersed throughout Asia, and possibly Europe and Australasia, prior to the evolution of modern *Homo sapiens* (conventionally dated to at least 70,000 possibly 150,000 years ago). Such genetic variations include Neanderthals, Peking Man, Java Man and *Homo floresiensis*, the tiny three-foot tall proto-human discovered in Indonesia in 2004 (all local subspecies of *Homo erectus*).

The multiregional hypothesis was originally developed from the fossil evidence, but more recent work has focused on molecular data, in which the DNA is sequenced.

Proponents of multiregionalism believe the molecular data can not only be reconciled with the multiregional origin hypothesis but in fact in some cases supports it. For instance, studies on past population bottlenecks that can be inferred from molecular data have led them to conclude that the single-origin hypothesis is untenable. One of the co-authors of a 1999 study, proponent John Hawks, is quoted as saying the single-origin theory 'can be put to rest'.

THE CHURCH'S DILEMMA
In 1950 Pope Pius XII published his encyclical *Humani Generis*. In it he said:

'The faithful cannot lend support to a theory [polygenism] which involves either the existence on this Earth, after Adam, of true men who would not originate from him, as the ancestor of all, by natural generation, or that 'Adam' stands for a plurality of ancestors. For it is not at all apparent how such a view can be reconciled with the data which the sources of revealed truth and the documents of the Church propose concerning Original Sin, namely, that it originates from a sin truly committed by one Adam, is transmitted to all through generation and is in each, proper to him.'

That a belief in the evolution of lower forms of life into higher forms of life does not contradict any teaching of the Church, was pointed out by Pope Pius XII in the above encyclical. More recently, in slightly stronger terms, Pope John Paul II, addressing the Pontifical Academy of Sciences in 1996, said: 'Today, almost half a century after the publication of the encyclical, new knowledge has led to the recognition of the theory of evolution as more than a hypothesis. However, the belief that Adam and Eve were not two individual human beings from whom all human beings descended does contradict what the Church teaches. Any hypothesis to the contrary would undermine Christian belief in the nature and transmission of Original Sin'.

The Catechism of the Catholic Church (1994) warns:

[The Church] knows very well that we cannot tamper with the revelation of Original Sin without undermining the mystery of Christ (No.389). The account of the Fall in Genesis 3 uses figurative language, but affirms a primeval event, a deed that took place at the beginning of the history of man. Revelation gives us certainty of faith that the whole of human history is marked by the original fault freely committed by our first parents (No.390).

Even allowing that the whole human race owes its origins to an evolutionary event in Africa, the dilemma with which the Church is faced is how to explain that all humanity is born with Original Sin other than by believing that the Original Sin was committed by a first ancestor who was as fully human as we are,

The Catechism of the Catholic Church also teaches that every spiritual soul is created immediately by God (No.366).John Paul II reiterated the words of Pius XII: 'If the human body takes its origin from pre-existent living matter, the spiritual soul is immediately created by God. Consequently, theories of evolution which, in accordance with the philosophies inspiring them, consider the spirit as emerging from the forces of living matter .... are incompatible with the truth about man'.

We know that life evolved from a single cell to *Homo sapiens* over a period of 3.5 billion years. *Homo habilis* (skilful person) emerged 2 million years ago, Neanderthals emerged 125,000 years ago and *Homo sapiens* as a fully evolved human being emerged in Africa around 100,000 years ago. At what point can we say our ancestors crossed the 'ontological gap' – the jump between a species with no eternal soul to ourselves with such a soul? When was the moment of human evolution when God created each individual soul? Can the earliest forms of human life, at which point there was a minimum of communication between creatures, be called human in the sense in which we understand that meaning today? Did such creatures have a human soul? At which point on this timescale of human emergence would one place a mythical Adam and the consequential Fall of humanity? Or, philosophers would ask, at what point in the great unfolding of evolution did human consciousness first appear?

Church teaching is based on two passages of St Paul. Namely, Romans 5: 2-19 in which Paul writes: 'Sin came into the world through one man and his sin brought death with it'. And: 'Just as all men die in Adam, so all men will be brought to life in Christ' (I Corinthians 15:22). The 'one man' Paul is referring to in Romans is Adam. In his time it was believed that Adam was an historical person, the first human being. The word 'one' was occasioned by the view of world history that existed in Paul's time. The majority of Scripture scholars today would say that Paul's reference to Adam is not in order to make a statement about our origins but to emphasise that just as sin and death ruled over humanity so grace and eternal life was restored through one person, namely through Jesus.

Although I have spelt out the dilemma as it challenges the Catholic Church, because this is the Church I know best as my ecclesiastical home, to have to rethink a theology of the soul, Original Sin and the role of Jesus as a saviour, in the light of emerging knowledge, is so fundamental to Christian belief that it is a dilemma that faces Churches of all denominations.

WHITHER ORIGINAL SIN?

Our uncertainty about our human evolution remains – whether *homo sapiens* evolved from one pair of human beings or not. If not, the notion of Original Sin has to be re-thought as an explanation for our human propensity for evil and it calls into question the salvific role of Jesus the Christ if we think of this in terms of repairing a past Fall. (We shall be looking at this in a later chapter.)

Soul talk is Church talk. St Paul speaks of our being body, mind and spirit (I Thessalonians 5:23). Spirit is consciousness, self-awareness. While some scientists still hold that our consciousness is dependent upon our physical brain, those who have researched out-of-the-body and near-death experiences of people, agree that our consciousness is not dependent upon our physical body. Those who believe in life after death claim that it is our consciousness which continues (into other realms?) or re-incarnates.

While we just do not know at what point in the great unfolding of evolution consciousness first appeared (indeed, in what sense can we speak, as some do, of rocks being conscious? Brains are not necessary for consciousness. A plant has no brain but has a consciousness) it is helpful to think of the evolution of human consciousness as happening in three stages. The first we can name Simple Consciousness. This is the state of non-differential awareness, what we might call the Eden state, where humanity, without a sense of space or time, lived in the present moment – as animals do today – not understanding themselves as separate beings from other beings. Then our ancestors came to the state of Self-consciousness around 300,000 years ago. Aware of themselves as distinct self-reflective individuals, the way was open for the development of language, reason, a sense of history and religion. There are many today who believe humanity is taking a third evolutionary step into Cosmic Consciousness, sometimes called Christ or Brahmic Consciousness: the consciousness of the mystics.

Studies of the human brain suggest that for any given human individual, only a fraction of the brain – approximately 10% - is used. Is the 90% being held in readiness for our next stage of evolution to *Homo luminus, Homo spiritus*?

6. THE COSMIC CHRIST: THE DIVINE ENERGY

By the Cosmic Christ we refer to the divine energy, perpetually creating and sustaining the Universe: the universal energy of love, the presence of the Divine in the Universe.

It is in the light of our emerging world view that we are led to reconsider what we mean by 'the Christ', especially in relation to the person of Jesus of Nazareth. Of all the factors composing our world view, that are causing Christians to rethink their notion of the Christ, I suggest that the predominant factor is our present understanding of evolution. Whether or not we accept the manner of its happening as proposed by Darwin - by the survival of the fittest - the fact of evolution of our species is now more than a hypothesis. It has caused our world view to change from the static to the dynamic; everything is continually in a process of change. Ideas, theories, doctrines, beliefs too are in constant process of change, no longer set in concrete for all eternity.

In respect of our particular subject this new world view has two implications. The first is that it challenges a traditional Christian belief in an interventionist God. Namely, that God intervened deliberately at some moment in history to create a human being, *Homo sapiens*. As we saw in the chapter on Creation, our early ancestors, *Homo habilis* (skilful man) emerged two million years ago and developed various strains – Neanderthals, Peking man, Java man, *Homo floresiensis* – all local sub-species of *Homo erectus*. At what point, we asked, can we claim that God intervened in the evolutionary process to insert an eternal soul?

Secondly, it challenges our belief that there was another direct intervention by God at a later point in history when the second person of the Trinity 'came down from heaven, by the power of the Holy Spirit, became incarnate from the Virgin Mary and was made man' (to quote the Nicene Creed).

In our present evolving world view the Jesus event can no longer be understood as causing a new creation, meaning putting right a first creation that an original pair of human beings damaged, but rather as a new event in a continuing creation process of which we are the most recent products. Even St Paul, knowing nothing about evolution, acknowledged our incompleteness and our journeying towards a final destiny (Romans 8:22-23).

That Jesus of Nazareth was an historical person living in Palestine at the beginning of our Common Era - AD as Christians designate it - is widely accepted by historians as well as Scripture scholars. It is about his being entitled the Christ and the relationship of the Christ to the Godhead that has caused theologians from the earliest years of the Church to debate, theorise and hold Councils. The relationship between the Jesus of history and the Christ of faith (or the Christ of dogma, as some say) continues to present a mystery upon which I shall try to throw some light. (By 'mystery' I mean that truth which in its totality we are unable to comprehend. We can only enter it piecemeal and appreciate it partially.)

THE NAME

Our translations into English of St Paul's letters, originally written in Greek, have their author write of 'Jesus Christ' as if a first name and a surname. And preachers and writers have used this appellation down to this day. It is fundamental to our re-thinking this mystery, that we recognise that 'Jesus' is the name of a human being born in history, while 'Christ' is a title given to that man. Etymologically, the word Christ, from the Greek, means the anointed one and as such has come to be associated with the Hebrew word 'Messiah' although its use in the sense of Messiah is extremely rare. In my own preaching and writing, as here, I always refer to 'Jesus the Christ'.

I understand the word Christ to have a much broader meaning: to be the manifestation of the Divine in creation. The Christ-life is the life of God lived as a human person. St Paul wrote: 'The Christ is the visible image of the invisible God' (Colossians 1:15) and elsewhere he speaks of 'the glory of the Christ who is the exact likeness of God' (2 Corinthians 4:4). Dom Bede Griffiths referred to the Christ as 'the icon of God'.

So no one can claim that the Christ is only Jesus. The Christ is more than Jesus, indeed more than a human person, however divine that person is conceived to be. Consequently to say that Jesus is the Christ is not the same as to say the Christ is solely Jesus. In other words, Jesus is the Christ, but the Christ is the Divine however and wherever the Divine is made manifest.

THE ETERNAL CHRIST

The Christ is God in creation: the creative Word, the Logos. So John's gospel begins:

'Before the world was created, the Word already existed; the Word was with God and the Word was God. From the very beginning the Word was with God. Through the Word God made all things; not one thing in all creation was made without Him. The Word was the source of life, and this life brought light to all humanity' (John 1:1-4).

This is more succinctly put by St Paul: 'Christ existed before all things and in union with Him all things have their proper place' (Colossians 1:17). The Word, the Christ, is God in the role of continuing creator, holding all things in being.

During the blessing of the Paschal Candle, the Easter Liturgy pronounces: 'Christ yesterday and today, the beginning and the end, Alpha and Omega; all time belongs to him, and all the ages; to him be glory and power, through every age and forever'. This is a way of saying the Christ is beyond time and space since both are a feature of our created Universe. 'Christ is all, Christ is in all' (Colossians 3:11).

Christ is not only the Alpha (the beginning) but also the Omega (the end) (Ephesians 1:10). Raimundo Panikkar writes in *The Unknown Christ of Hinduism*:

'This then is the Christ: that reality through whom everything has come, in whom everything subsists, to whom everything that suffers the wear and tear of time shall return. He is the embodiment of Divine Grace that leads everyone to God; there is no other way but through Him (John 14:6)'.

THE COSMIC CHRIST

To speak of the Christ is always to speak of the Cosmic Christ.

The Jesuit palaeontologist and mystic of the last century, Pierre Teilhard de Chardin, with his evolutionary vision of the world, presents the Christ as the physical centre of the world, of evolution, and gives three quotations from St Paul to support his view:

Romans 8:19-23 (the whole creation is groaning until now in an agony of birth)
Colossians 1:15-20 (the pre-existence of the Christ 'born before every creation')
Ephesians 1:9-10, 22-23 (God's design from the beginning centred in the Christ).
(Quoted by Christopher F. Mooney in *Teilhard de Chardin and the Mystery of Christ*.)

THE CHRIST IN RELATION TO HUMANITY

For us human beings the Christ can never be totally known on Earth because to see Christ would amount to 'seeing the Father' (John 14:9), to comprehending the Godhead.

As human beings we can only think of God in human terms. We can do no other. This limited human concept of the Christ I shall call 'the Christ myth'. (A myth is not a non-reality, but rather the expression, through image or story, of a truth which is beyond our total comprehension, beyond verbal description.) For us as human beings the highest expression of the Christ myth is in human form. It expresses the archetypal image of the fully mature human being: the person as God-like as it is possible for a human being to become. That ideal person who, in our deepest selves, we all aspire to become. So there are many manifestations of the Christ myth. Indeed, every one of us, whether recognising it or not, is to a greater or lesser extent, at different times, no doubt, an image, a reflection of the Christ: an embodiment of the Christ. This recognition came to St Paul: 'It is no longer I who live but it is the Christ who lives in me' (Galatians 2:20) and elsewhere he writes: 'The secret is that Christ is in you, which means that you will share in the glory of God' (Colossians 1:27). Paul writes 'in Christ' 165 times in his letters and the virtually synonymous 'in the Spirit' some 20 times. There are not many Christs but only the one Christ and many manifestations of that one Christ.

JESUS THE CHRIST

The manifestation of the Christ with which Christians are most familiar is in the human person of Jesus of Nazareth. We think of him as the most complete, the most God-like, most God-filled human being. While the Christ pre-existed the Universe, Jesus of Nazareth did not. He 'dwelt among us' in one short period of human history. While Jesus lived in Palestine - supposedly for some thirty years - there was not an absence of the Christ within the Godhead during that period! The pre-existent Christ is in the Godhead eternally, without interruption: what we name the Son, the second Person of the Trinity.

The man Jesus was a product of millions of years of evolution. While there was no need of his having a miraculous birth in the biological sense, the myth of such a miraculous birth states the truth that Jesus was a very special person. In what way special? Whatever may have been the view of the Gospel writers, a contemporary way of answering this question is to say that Jesus can be recognised as the first fully mature man in our western culture: a 'new man' in whom the highest form of consciousness - Christ consciousness - has broken through. St Paul calls Jesus 'the second Adam' or 'the last Adam': 'The last Adam is the life-giving Spirit' (I Corinthians 15:45).

The Spirit can blossom fully within humanity when we are prepared to let go of the pre-resurrection Jesus and give space to the Cosmic Christ. On the last day of the Jewish Festival of Tabernacles, Jesus was speaking about the Spirit which those who believed in him would receive. To this report John's Gospel adds the note: 'At that time the Spirit had not yet been given, because Jesus had not been raised to glory' (7:39). And speaking to his closest friends just before his death, Jesus said: 'It is better for you that I go away, because if I do not go, the Helper [Spirit] will not come to you' (John 16:7).

Christian tradition speaks of Jesus' coming as the 'Incarnation', meaning that the person of Jesus pre-existed time. In an evolutionary perspective, the very first human beings - those primates which evolved into creatures with which we can identify - were the first creatures to develop a self-reflective consciousness, and consequently the first to have the potential to recognise the Divine in nature. In this sense we can say they were the first Incarnation of the Christ. The Jesus event, a million or more years later, was the achievement of humanity reaching its incarnational maturity. (The feast of Christmas is the celebration of this achievement.) Jesus was not a being different in kind from us, launched into our world from some heavenly abode, but a product like us of the evolutionary process, which is why I speak of the Jesus event as a human achievement. And yet, 2000 years later, the rest of us are still in a pre-Christian era, striving to evolve to the heights of the Christ myth.

However, the person of Jesus is more than a model of what we might become. In Christian terminology, as we have already said, 'Christ' means the anointed one, the specially chosen of God, and variously called Messiah, Saviour. Jesus, by his being the very fulfilment of the archetypal human being, breaks through the barriers of human limitation and thereby empowers us to follow in the same 'Way' (as we shall see in a forthcoming chapter). He was so completely for others, living entirely for the Divine Other, that the Christ within him was released to full capacity. The powers he is reported to have exercised - physical healing, spiritual healing, power over nature and material things - he was able to do, not because he was God, but because he was a fully evolved human being 'reaching to the very height of the Christ's full stature' (Ephesians 4:13), as Luke says: 'The power of the Spirit was with him' (4:14). He is the New Adam, in that he broke through to a new level of consciousness, into the next evolutionary step for humanity. Jesus promised us 'Whoever believes in me will do what I do - yes, he will do even greater things' (John 14:12). The Kingdom message of Jesus - the very kernel of his teaching - supposes that humanity is, through him, evolving into a new consciousness, a fuller life. 'I have come in order that you might have life, life in all its fullness', said Jesus (John 10:10). The Christ, acting in the world as creative energy, initiates our evolution as creatures of the Spirit. 'If Christ lives in you, the Spirit is life for you' (Romans 8:10). (In other translations: 'If the Christ lives in you, your spirit is alive'.)

What we call the resurrection of Jesus is the symbol of the newly constituted human creature: that state which humanity will evolve into. Just as at our death we shed our human body as being no longer required, so after his death Jesus no longer required his human body, except in a form by which to make known to his disciples that he still lived, though in a higher form of life. Thus his resurrected 'body' had different properties from our physical bodies.

A literal belief in the resurrection appearances tells us nothing about 'life after death'. Jesus told us nothing about the nature of his post-resurrection life, nor do we know what became of the human Jesus after he was seen for the last time. If at some future date archaeologists find the remains of a body in a Jerusalem tomb that could be identified as that of Jesus of Nazareth, it would not make the slightest difference to belief in Jesus as the Christ.

A BRIEF HISTORY

In this chapter it is not possible to trace the development of the Christ myth through the 2000 years of Hebrew history, but Jesus was a child of this myth and it was in its light that the Apostles interpreted who Jesus was and so gave meaning to his death and resurrection.

Jesus was born into a religion and culture fully expecting the appearance of a Messiah. Although understanding themselves as a Chosen People, the children of Israel had had their nation divided, banished into exile and now occupied by a foreign and pagan empire. Living in fear of a permanent loss of identity, the Jews of Jesus' time longed for a king and a kingdom which reflected the glorious days of King David. These were the expectations and longings amidst which the young Jesus grew up. Just as with every human being, Jesus' knowledge of God and God's intentions could only come from his own experience and that of other people. He would have been well grounded in the Hebrew Scriptures, familiar with his people's stories, myths, poetry and prophecies. Did Jesus actually think of himself as the expected Messiah? Certainly he did not identify with the myth of a son of David restoring an earthly kingdom to Israel. Yet when Nathanael greets him with: 'Rabbi, you are the Son of God, you are the King of Israel' (John 1:49) Jesus does not deny this exalted epithet. He understood that his mission centred around proclaiming the Kingdom of God which was both an inner experience (John 3:3) and a sociological vision: the world as God meant it to be. He spoke as 'one having authority' (Matthew 7:28) because he lived by the Kingdom values which he preached.

What began as a Messiah myth embodying the expectations of a saviour of the Jewish people as a nation, evolved into a Christ myth proclaiming a universal saviour for all humanity, identified as Jesus of Nazareth.

Since the earliest days of the Church - as soon as it spread into the Greek world - the Good News of the Gospel began to be expressed in terms of Greek culture. Philosophical controversies arose. For the first six centuries of Christian history there was endless debate over whether Jesus was fully human but had become divine or fully God but took on a human nature, or whether he was a person of two equal natures, human and divine at the same time. Docetism (a heresy in the early Church that the humanity of Jesus, his sufferings and death were only apparent, not real) underplayed his humanity; while Arianism (another heresy which asserted that Jesus was not of one substance with the Father) did not do justice to his divinity. What was the nature of this union? How could two natures be integrated in the one person? To make the distinction between a divine nature and a human nature in Jesus is to create a dualism that implies that it is beyond our own capacity with our human nature and its insufficiently focused consciousness, to be open to the realisation of the Divine within us as Jesus was.

JESUS' RELATIONSHIP WITH GOD

From John's account of Jesus sharing his deepest self with his closest friends at the Last Supper it is clear that he experienced a very close intimacy - what today we would call Unity Consciousness - with God.

Every person has the presence of the Divine within them. As the Quakers say: 'There is that of God in all men'. What distinguishes us from each other is our level of awareness of this presence and consequently the degree of our ability to draw on the potential divine energy. All of us are sons or daughters of God. The Christ within Jesus is the same Christ within us. 'Your real life is Christ', wrote Paul to the Christians in Colossae (3:4). The difference is one of degree, not of kind. (This idea appeared in the early Church and was called *Adoptionism*. It was condemned by the Council of Nicaea (325) that declared that the difference between Jesus and other human beings was one of kind (Jesus alone was Divine), not of degree. But no statement of Truth is absolute for all time.) *

In raising humanity to a new level of awareness of our human-God relationship, Jesus as the Christ would have us dispense with religion's intermediaries and communicate with God directly. 'In union with the Christ and through our faith in Him we have the boldness to go into God's presence with all confidence' (Ephesians 3:13). That presence is within us. The God who dwells deep within us is much more magnificent than the distant Sky God of religious myth. We worship the God to which the Christ myth points, whom we see reflected in the man Jesus. We do not worship the historical Jesus in himself.

In the Eucharist is celebrated one of the modes of the presence of the Christ, under the forms of bread and wine, without identifying it with the historical, biological body and blood of the human Jesus. In administering Holy Communion the minister proclaims: 'The Body of Christ'. This acknowledges that we form 'the body of Christ' (Ephesians 1:23), and are called 'to build up the body of Christ' (Ephesians 4:12).

FUTURE HOPE
While Christians claim to be followers of Jesus as the Christ, because he is the most perfect expression of what we aspire to become, we have to recognise that the Christ myth has its counterpart in other Faiths, as the ideal to which humanity aspires, whether in the

---

* An increasing number of contemporary theologians (John Robinson, John Macquarrie among them), because they maintain a panentheistic view of the God-creation relationship, think of Jesus as different from other persons by degree rather than kind.

form of 'the way' of Lao-tzu in Taoism or the Bodhisattva (the saviour figure in Buddhism) or the Quetzalcoatl myth of the Aztecs.

When the Apostles said (Acts 4:12): 'There is no other name by which we can be saved' they were not ruling out the possibility of other saviours, but proclaiming that it was not they but their risen Lord - the eternal Christ - who was working such wonders.

If with this understanding of the Christ in our present world view we are able to make a distinction between the historical Jesus of Nazareth and the Christ of faith, might this not be a basis of dialogue between the great world religions? Islam holds Jesus in high regard, not as divine, but as a prophet. Enter the home of a Hindu and you are likely to find in their shrine a picture of Jesus alongside Kali, Vishnu and Shiva. Jesus for them is one of many expressions of the manifold qualities of the Divine.

What our world needs to move towards is a shared understanding of what it means to manifest the Divine life. For this purpose, the concept of the cosmic or universal Christ is fundamental.

7. TAPPING DIVINE ENERGY

The first word that would come to most Christians' minds, if asked how they might tap divine energy, would be 'prayer'.

Again, for many people, asked what prayer is, they would think of petitionary prayer. Pray is what you do when you want something badly; to be saved from a situation, to supply an immediate need, to cure a friend's illness, to reduce suffering. How often we hear of people who would never think of prayer as a daily exercise, only appealing to 'someone up there' as a last resort in a crisis.

What do they expect the God-up-there to do? To bend the laws of nature for their benefit? To perform a miracle? Chesterton said God is the most useless of all beings. The one Being we cannot use. He is not 'up there' to bring about our every whim. In his first papal encyclical letter (2006) Pope Benedict XVI wrote: 'The Christian who prays does not claim to be able to change God's plans or correct what He has foreseen'.

But then there are other forms of prayer besides intercessionary prayer. There are prayers of praise, of thanksgiving. These can be prayed in private or in a community as in worship, in the liturgy or in performing a ritual. We might regard all the above as 'saying' prayers. They are all different forms that 'talking to God' might take. But they are not the essence of prayer. Prayer is an act of the will: the will to be in communication with God, which implies listening as much as speaking.

God does not need our praise or worship. He does not feel better for our doing it. We might. But there is a danger that in saying prayers we are maintaining ourselves in a relationship with a theistic interventionist God. When, in petitionary prayer, we pray for our own needs, we should not be expecting God to obey our wishes, but we are disposing ourselves to the will of God, to accept to go with the flow of the evolutionary current. If we are praying for the healing of others - either for the health of persons or for peace in a suffering situation - then we are directing the healing energies of God through The Field to that person or situation.

So tapping divine energy through prayer, implies not only being active (saying prayers) but being actively passive: being aware of God's presence within us. This requires stillness, which is the purpose of all the different methods of meditation. To be still is to live the present moment.

A clarification is needed about the word 'meditation'. It can take two forms. In the Western ascetical tradition we use the word 'meditation' to mean a discursive activity, where one uses the rational mind to ponder a verse of Scripture, a favourite hymn, or to imagine oneself taking part in a gospel scene - as in Ignation meditation. We use the word 'contemplation' to describe being actively passive: just 'being' with an awareness of God, being open to allow the Spirit to act, not through our rational mind but through intuition, inspiration. The former may give us a greater knowledge *about* God and the sacred mysteries, while the latter gives us an experience *of*

EXPRESSIONS OF LOVE IN THE WORLD'S GREAT RELIGIONS

BAHAI	Love Me that I may love thee. If thou lovest Me not, My love can no wise reach thee.
BUDDHISM	Let each one of us cultivate towards the whole world a heart of love.
CHRISTIANITY	Beloved, let us love one another, for love is of God.
CONFUCIANISM	To love all is the greatest benevolence.
HINDUISM	One can best worship the Lord through love.
ISLAM	Love is this, that thou shouldst account thyself very little and God very great.
JAINISM	The days are of most profit to those who act in love.
JUDAISM	Thou shalt love the Lord thy God with all thy heart, and thy neighbour as thyself.
SHINTO	Love is the representative of the Lord.
SIKHISM	God will regenerate those in whose hearts there is love.
TAOISM	Heaven arms with love those it would not see destroyed.
ZOROASTRIANISM	Wo/man is the beloved if the Lord and should love in return.

God.

Confusion arises because the eastern religions use the two words meditation and contemplation in exactly the other way round! Today, the advertisements we see offering to teach us methods of meditation are using the word in the eastern sense. This is how it is commonly used in the West today outside church circles. This is how we will use the word here.

Just as all prayer is not meditation, so not all meditation is prayer. For it to be prayer depends upon the intention of the one meditating. I have met many meditators who have no roots in any religious tradition but who have adopted the practice for health reasons (perhaps on the suggestion of their doctor to lower their blood pressure) or for intellectual reasons: to become more creative, to improve their memory. Because meditating is a holistic practice, for whatever reason one might have started meditating, one effect will be the stimulation of one's spiritual dimension which may have lain dormant. No matter what a person's intention is in meditating, the practice will draw them into an altered state of consciousness – the brain shifts to lower frequencies – which causes a greater output of energy, which in turn affects their surroundings.

MEDITATION IS COSMIC

Worship is directed by us, individually or collectively, to God alone. Meditation, on the other hand, is communion with God in the context of the whole cosmos. The former is directed to God beyond creation; the latter to God within creation - it is panentheistic. In our intercessions we pray with expecta-

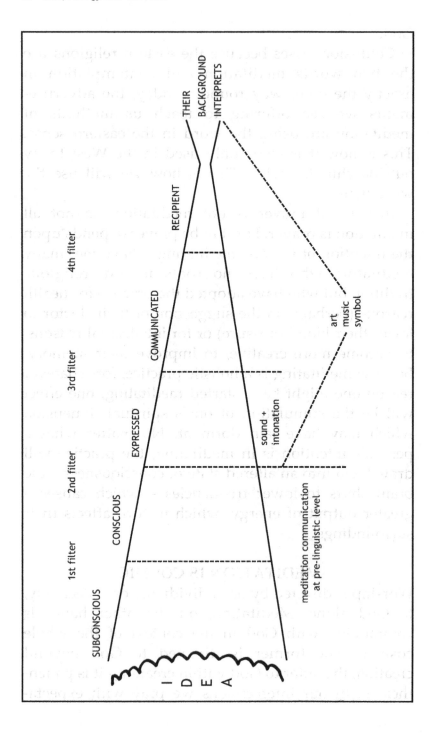

tions, in meditation we have none. In fact the golden rule in all forms of meditation is: 'don't try: just do it'.

When we attempt to communicate our thoughts to another, the communication process passes through a number of filters, each of which diminishes the power of the original thought. (See diagram on next page.) The thought originates in our sub-consciousness but it is already diminished when we bring it into our consciousness and more so when we use words to express it to ourselves. We then attempt to communicate this expressed thought to someone else, but what they receive is filtered still further by the way their background interprets it. The most obstructive filter is when the communication is made between different languages.

But words are not the only means of communication. Ideas are also communicated, with less filters, through art, music and symbol. In meditation our communication with the Divine is at the pre-linguistic stage, where our intercourse is not the transmission of information but the sharing of consciousness, and this sharing of consciousness is two-way.

In the chapter on The Field we spoke about the four fundamental forces of nature: the electro-magnetic, the weak interaction, the strong interaction and gravitation and the search by scientists to come up with a Grand Unified Theory to explain them all. But this is at the intellectual level of physics. In meditation one has a direct experience of the unified field of pure consciousness.

THE COHERENCE FIELD
At this level, a group of people meditating together, build up a field of coherence. Quantum physics has

made us aware that everything, every being, is inter-connected and interdependent. Thus this field of coherence not only enhances the consciousness of the meditators themselves (meditators claim that it is much easier to meditate in a group than alone) but also affects the neighbourhood. The meditation is the most powerful way of tapping divine energy, for both personal and collective benefit. Monitoring of meditation has shown that one effect is the reduction of stress.

There have been many scientific researches carried out over the last three decades on behalf of the Transcendental Meditation movement, which reveal the effect on city life, and even national life, brought about when a sufficient number (1% of a population) meditate as a group. The effect of reduced stress can be measured by the reduction in the crime rate, less homicide and traffic fatalities, a lowering in the number of hospital admissions, over a given period.

Here is one example of the power of synchronised group meditation. It was in November 1978, while I was living in Zambia, that there was a civil war being fought in next-door Rhodesia between the white settler and the black indigenous populations because their leader, Ian Smith, had declared unilateral independence from British sovereignty. Maharishi Mahesh Yogi, who had brought Transcendental Meditation to the West, despatched forty people practising the advanced form of TM to the capital, Salisbury, with instructions to do intensive periods of meditation each day. There were two outcomes worthy of note. Once they began, the average number of deaths daily due to the fighting dropped from 26 to 4, rural people returned to normal life and schools, which had been closed due to guerrilla activities reopened. The second noteworthy feature is that after ten days the group of forty decided they would be more effective if half of them were to go to the second major city, Bulawayo, two hundred miles away, with the purpose of spreading their influence. In fact it had the opposite of the desired effect. During those ten days the average number of war deaths rose to ten a day. When their visitor's visas expired and they had to leave, the number of war deaths rose again to an average of 26 per day.

DISTANT HEALING

To return to petitionary prayer, what do we believe happens when we pray to God for healing, for example? Or rather, how do we explain a desired effect coming about if it is not through direct divine intervention? As Larry Dossey says in *HealingWords*: 'The most persuasive reason to believe that prayer works is the indisputable fact that everyone uses it, pagans and orthodox believers alike'. Dossey, a medical doctor, is only one among many who, in recent years, have carried out tests to judge the efficacy of prayer. One 'experiment' has become widely known. It was carried out by a cardiologist Randolph Byrd, a practising Christian. The test was carried out over a ten-month period in the coronary care unit of San Francisco General Hospital. He arranged for 192 patients to be prayed for by individuals or prayer groups. 201 patients were not prayed for. It was a double-blind experiment in which neither the patients, nurses nor doctors knew who was and who was not being prayed for. The prayer groups were given the first names of their patients as well as a brief description of their condition. They were asked to pray each day but given no instruction on how or what to pray for. Each patient had between five and seven people praying for them. Byrd lists, in medical terms, the benefits received by those who were prayed for as against those who were not. The effect was so impressive that it was said that if the technique being studied had been a new drug or surgical procedure instead of prayer, it would have been announced as a 'breakthrough'.

Another occasion illustrating the effect of group prayer is given by Gregg Braden in his book *The Isaiah Effect*. This was on November 13, 1998, the final day of the time-limit imposed on Iraq to comply with the United Nations demand for inspection of its supposed weapons of mass-destruction. Iraq was threatened that non-compliance would result in a bombing campaign to destroy suspected weapons sites. The result, inevitably, would have meant a great loss of life, probably civilian as well as military. Through the Internet several hundred thousand people in at least thirty-five countries on six continents, were implored to pray for peace at a precise time on that evening of November 13. Gregg Braden writes: 'Thirty minutes into the aerial attack, the President of the United States, having received a letter from the Iraqi officials stating that they would now cooperate with the requested weapons inspection, issued a rare order to the U.S. forces to "stand down", the military term for aborting the mission.' The situation was saved, not by an anti-war demonstration but a mass will for peace whose effect it is difficult to discredit. An overpowering energy for peace had had a positive effect through The Field.

TRANSMITTING ENERGY

We might call these phenomena the sociological, as different from personal, benefit of healing prayer and meditation. The difference between prayer and meditation in their intention is that the former is directed to the needs of a particular person or area of conflict, while meditation causes a general de-stressing of the surroundings without any effect being willed directly. In both cases creative energy is drawn upon and disseminated through The Field.

Healing energy can be transmitted even unconsciously. When my father was living in a Home for the elderly in his last years, I would often spend a day with him, perhaps taking him out for a meal or a run in the car. We got on famously together, but by the end of the day I felt completely drained of energy. Without either of us being aware of it, his frailty was sucking energy from my healthy body. There was an unconscious transference of energy taking place through The Field.

The sacraments are a ritual for the transference of energy. It is noticeable that each of the seven sacraments is bestowed in a one-to-one form, sometimes with the laying on of hands, other times using symbols, of water, oil, bread and wine.

Sad to say, we humans can also cause harm, the opposite of healing, through our influence on the energies around us. Just as a large group of meditators can reduce stress in their vicinity, so a crowd of people causing disharmony can affect negatively the physical energies.

We will say more on the subject of the negative effects of energy in the chapter on evil.

8. EVIL AS MISUSED ENERGY

On many occasions I have astonished my audiences by declaring that the announcement of the bad news of what humans inflict on other humans - murders, muggings, racial cleansing, genocide, and such like - is for me a great assurance that all is well with our world! I hasten to stress the word 'announcement'. It is not the brutality which gives me heart but the fact that such events are thought to be news-worthy. What makes news is that which is the exception to normality. That these atrocities still make news confirms to me two things: that what is normal, most frequent, all-pervading in our world, is goodness. Secondly, that people's values are good and positive and their expectation is of peace and harmony. Yes, humanity is basically good. Sadly, it is only too easy to believe, when we are bombarded by the media each day with so much negativity, that humanity is becoming increasingly evil, uncaring, criminal and vicious. I do not believe that humanity is any more vicious today than, for instance, in biblical times or in the Middle Ages. There is quantitatively more evil abroad because there are more human beings around, but not more qualitatively.

No human being can pass through life without experiencing the effects of evil, either in what affects them personally or in the surroundings. But what is evil? It is a coincidence that in English *evil* is *live* spelt backwards! Evil is all that which is anti-life, anti-growth, whether it be damaging to our personal growth towards fulfilment or preventing the growth of other people or hampering the evolution of our Planet Earth: disrespect for the integrity of creation. The imbalance between the wealth and power of the Northern Hemisphere and the poverty and depression of the Southern Hemisphere causes a massive imbalance of energy in the body of our planetary energy field.

Does evil have an identifiable essence? Is it negative energy? We have already said that since all energy emanates from God, all energy is good. So what we might think of as negative energy, evil, is in fact energy misused by us human beings.

There are some who attempt to give substance to evil by personifying it in the form of devils, Satan, evil spirits, onto whom they can shift blame for their own wrong choices. A classical example of that is the reply Eve gave in the garden of Eden story. Adam having blamed her for leading them astray, she in turn blamed the serpent (Genesis 3:12-13). Fear of punishment, reprisal, turns an adult into a child, making excuses, shifting responsibility onto an event, an object, another person, a snake, even!

Evil is not an entity in itself. Compare it to a hole. We all know what a hole is, we can fall into it and break our neck. Yet there is no such thing as a hole. I cannot go to the DIY shop and order a swimming pool 20x10 metres. A hole is an absence of whatever surrounds it. Like evil, it has no existence of its own: it is a negativity. We each have our shadow side. We need no convincing of that. It has to be acknowledged just as much as our goodness. The Chinese speak of the balance that has to be kept between the Yin and the Yang.

ANIMALS CAN DO NO EVIL

This is not just so in human life but in all of nature. We notice negativity - we might mistakenly call it evil - present in the animal kingdom. For instance, hyenas usually have twins but invariably within minutes of birth one of the cubs attacks its twin, and it is a fight to the death. The cuckoo is well known for poaching other bird's nests to lay its own eggs, sometimes destroying the host's clutch of eggs.

In all these cases these creatures are acting according to their nature, not by free choice. Animals are not capable of evil. Evil belongs only to the human domain. Animals cannot make mistakes. They always do the right thing according to their nature.

'But what cruelty' we say as we watch a TV documentary of the Serengeti Plain of East Africa, seeing a leopard pouncing on a young gazelle and tearing it to pieces with her teeth. 'What suffering the leopard is inflicting', or is she? The names we give to all these 'cruel', 'wicked' acts - infanticide, cannibalism, rape, conquest, deception, murder - are a projection of our human moral code onto the animal world. We give such actions these names because for us, with our ability to choose, we rightly condemn such activities in human life as evil. We measure them against our own scale of social values. And as we will see later, we have built up this scale of values from the experience of our ancestors and confirmed by our own experience, according to what we are required to do, and what to avoid, if we human beings are to live in harmony together in our particular culture.

We need to distinguish between pain and suffering. Pain is physical. Suffering is in the mind: it is the mental process set off by experiencing pain in the body. While all conscious beings, all creatures of the animal kingdom, can experience pain, only we with our ability for reflective consciousness, can suffer. It is caused by our thinking about pain: our fear that it might happen, our worry that it will be prolonged. This is because only we creatures have the mental ability to place ourselves in a present situation in relation to a past and a future. Only we have a sense of time and duration. The rest of the animal kingdom only has a consciousness of the present. They live in a perpetual NOW moment. Our suffering comes from our reflecting upon the pain and particularly on how long it may last and the consequences. This is what Eckhart Tolle means when he says: what we suffer from is not pain but our sense of time.

DEATH

We fear dying only because we have a sense of the future. Animals are unable to think about death and consequently have no fear of dying. It was the same with our early ancestors in their transition stage from primates to *Homo sapiens* – the self-reflective human as we know her. They lived in a state that the first book of the Bible described as the Garden of Eden or Paradise. As with the primates of today, these ancestors had no sense of differentiation either from their fellow creatures or from their surroundings. They felt at one with everything and at one with the present, without a sense of time or space. So they too did not suffer nor had they a fear of death: they were unable to anticipate it. This is why in the mythical biblical account of Adam and Eve's life in the Garden of Eden, God had told them that a consequence of their eating from 'the tree which gives knowledge of what is good and what is bad' (sometimes translated as: 'the tree that gives knowledge of everything') (Genesis 2:9, 16-17) would be that they would die (Genesis 3:3). As human beings they would naturally have aged and died anyway as all the animals do, but their eating the forbidden fruit, their acquiring 'knowledge of everything', included self-reflective consciousness and an experience of past and future, with consequent thoughts and fears of death.

PAIN AND SUFFERING
Pain - and in human terms, suffering - is part and parcel of the process of evolution. The 'cruel' actions of animals we listed above are part of their nature because they are necessary acts for their survival as a species. Such acts - for example those which control over-population by killing off some members of the pack - allow for the best conditions for the next generation.

But we must not be surprised to find the same or similar actions in tribes of human beings. Such practices as headhunting, ritual killing, may serve ecological equilibrium, stability of the population and social cohesion. Why do we humans treat some people as friends and some as enemies? It is usually because we experience an imbalance, whether it be of territory or wealth or resources, or when groups become too big to be manageable or too small to feel secure.

So we should not naively be too quick to classify all suffering, even that inflicted upon one section of humanity by another, as evil in intent. We have to recognise that pain, with its attendant suffering, is an inevitable part of human evolution too. There is the suffering of the mother in giving birth, while the baby experiences pain in being born because the large evolved head of a human baby has to descend a birth canal evolved for something smaller.

Pain has a positive value when, for instance, it acts as a warning signal. A toothache tells us our teeth need attention, a stomach ache warns us of over-eating or of eating something poisonous.

In the human domain we commonly regard all suffering as something to be avoided, and so label it 'evil'. But what we suffer, or suffer from, flows from a number of causes. There are natural phenomena such as plagues, earthquakes, famine, drought, floods, etc., which are often labelled evils but are in fact not evil but simply the cause of suffering. Then there are human causes of suffering such as pollution, war, torture, slavery, rape, nuclear bombs, ethnic cleansing, etc. These are humanly caused because their root lies within human nature: pride, greed, hate, desire for revenge, envy, jealousy, lust for power, prejudice, deceitfulness, etc.

Evil is confined to humanity on account of our ability to make choices.

Evil is not necessary but it is inevitable. Having the freedom to choose, we so often make the less perfect choice. We make mistakes. Viewing our wrong choices as mistakes can emphasise that our wrong-doing can be learnt from. Looked at in this way, there is a positive value concealed in that to which we would normally attribute a negative value.

RELATIVE VALUES

The values of good and evil are not absolute values. They vary from culture to culture. What might be judged good or allowable in one period of history can be judged wrong or evil in a later period. One can instance slavery, colonialism, capital punishment, witch hunts. What is experienced as barbaric by the recipients of certain actions, can be regarded as for the best by the perpetrators, as for example, the Inquisition, Apartheid, the Holocaust, ethnic cleansing. What is acceptable behaviour in one culture can be regarded as evil by another. The Mundurucu head-hunters of the Amazon regard outsiders as fair game for such hunting. It is justified by regarding the enemy as having an inferior status, on a par with animals.

We do not have to look very far back in western society to witness the domination of women by men. Before the suffragette movement their position of inferiority was recognised officially. Today, in theory there is equality but in practice this is not always so evident. The incidents of domestic violence, in which women are abused by men, that are reported to the police are only the tip of the iceberg. We can be thankful that in the West such relationships are not as violent or as organised as among the 10,000 strong Tanomamo tribe on the borders of Brazil and Venezuela. Here, the status of men is determined by their capacity for violence and their willingness to fight. The violence is almost always towards women. Battles between villages are sparked off by the abduction of a woman or by infidelity or adultery and end with the capture of women by the conquering team. The women are valued as commodities.

All of which raises the question: by what rules do human beings decide what is good and what is bad? For clearly there are no norms which are universally applicable to humanity. We are very quick to judge the behaviour of other cultures by the measure of our own. Judging the action leads to judging the perpetrator, which in turn leads to imputing blame. Blame never achieves anything except that of giving the one doing the blaming a feeling of moral superiority. Yet there is within our human nature a deep need to apportion blame even to the extent that if another human being cannot be blamed, we have recourse to a scapegoat. Leviticus (16:20-22) tells of the Israelites loading their collective guilt on an animal as a symbolic substitute for themselves, then driving it out into the desert to die.

So we come back to the question: from where do we get our sense of good and evil? Not from an outside God.

MORAL CODES

Religions have their own codes. But what is the source of these? Some appeal to divine revelation. So let us take as an example the Christian moral paradigm because it has been so influential in providing an ethical foundation for western society.

The Christian moral code was built upon that of the people of Israel. This in turn grew gradually from the ethical practice of the earliest tribes. Their religious history began some 4000 years ago with the call and journey of Abraham from Ur, where he was living by that people's social mores, to what became known as 'The Promised Land' where he put down his roots among another people with another culture. One of their customs was to sacrifice babies to their god Moloch. Palestine, even at that time, was a trading station, being a crossroads between the East and the West, between North and South. (Indian influence is found at an early date in Egypt.) While some of the Hebrews spent years in Egypt as slaves they picked up some of the Egyptian patterns of behaviour. It was when they escaped from years of slavery and were a people wandering around the desert of the Sinai Peninsula that their basic moral tenets became codified. This is described as Moses receiving the ten commandments directly from God - a divine revelation. They were to be for all time, to be inscribed on their hearts as if engraved in stone. But did it really happen as described in the book of Exodus (chapter 20) and Deuteronomy (chapter 5)? Were these precepts quite new? And how universal are they? The only precept which we can claim to be universal - the equiv-alent being found in all religions - is what is known as the Golden Rule: 'Love thy neighbour as thyself' or as Jesus said: 'Do for others what you want them to do for you: this is the meaning of the Law and the Prophets' (Matthew 7:12, Luke 6:31). It is sometimes expressed negatively: 'Do not do to others what you would not wish them to do to you'.

Our sense of right and wrong, of good and evil, has a human origin, originating in human experience of what fosters peaceful relationships and what does not. So we should not be surprised that our moral code of practice evolves. Among the recent-comers we can mention feminism as a concern to raise the general social value of women, environmentalism to raise our awareness of our treatment of our planet and of all living things that populate it, anti-racism to cause us to value other races than our own and increasing disgust at capital punishment. Moral systems develop from these values. Some are imposed by law, by command, and imposed on the many by the few, by the leaders. They are based on an ethic of obedience to authority.

And so we come to sin! What is sinful and what is not, is decreed to us by the religious hierarchy. Christians have been traditionally taught that a sin is an offence against God. The implication being that our sinfulness in some way saddens, hurts God, which of course is nonsense. We are incapable of affecting God's moods. If our relationship with God is dependent upon our being good or evil, the effect is entirely one-sided: on our side. It has no effect on God. To think it does is to maintain a personified view of God. So our understanding of sin is dependent upon our perception of God.

Any evil we do, in thought or in act, has its detrimental effect on ourselves or on other people or on nature, the environment. This is what sin is: that which prevents growth, in ourselves, of others or that militates against nature's evolutionary process. We can only say we offend God by analogy, in that we are being destructive of the ordering of creation in which God is present.

'The Spirit stands for progress, and evil, by definition then, is that which refuses progress' (Origen c.185 -c 254 CE).

9. AT-ONE-MENT THROUGH THE MORPHIC FIELD

Once human consciousness had evolved to the point where our early ancestors were able to differentiate themselves from their surroundings and from others, to establish a personal identity - leaving the Eden State, one might say - they began to disagree among themselves. This was inevitable because they thought for themselves and made personal choices. This is the point in human history where evil was born. Different choices led to disagreements, which led to arguments, which led to flights, which led to wars.

No sooner was there a realisation of this disaster upsetting the harmony in the family, the clan, than our ancestors looked for some way of addressing the root problem. This was a human problem because humans alone of all species have a free will. It is we humans who have become out of harmony not only with each other but with nature and it's evolving process. In different parts of the world different cultures began to offer different explanations for the cause of evil and also for a cure. Since each had open channels to their gods they did so in the context of their relationship to the transcendent world. So, different philosophies of life began to develop. We in the West call these philosophies 'religions' today. All religions stemmed from a sense of wrongness, of incapacity.

While all humanity had a common origin and has a

common destiny - whatever that may be - different understandings of the remedy for our faulty human condition emerged. We in the West are most familiar with the Jewish remedy - the expectation of a Saviour, a Redeemer, an idea which they had picked up from the Zoroastrians during their years in exile in Babylon.

EXPECTATIONS OF A MESSIAH

Other ideas which seeped into the Jewish religion during their seventy years - three generations - captivity in Babylon were the Zoroastrian belief in two primordial forces battling for control of the world, angels and devils, of a heaven and a hell as places of reward and punishment, of physical resurrection, a judgment at the end of time and, of particular concern to us here, their vision of a Messianic figure who would introduce a new era and overthrow the evil one.

It is not surprising then that at the time of Jesus they where expecting a Messiah who would rid them of the yoke of Roman occupation and return them to the glorious days of King David.

'Salvation' is the saving from what is wrong so as to access the better. For the Jews at that time salvation was not thought of as personal salvation but rather as salvation of the nation. As the Jesus form of Judaism began to spread and a different religion emerged - Christianity - the meaning of salvation became personal. It became salvation from the wrath of God, from divine punishment, to find its completion in access to a heavenly eternity. And this became accessible to believers, according to St Paul, through the passion, blood sacrifice and death of Jesus, the god-man, on a cross. It has been the Christian tradition to this day that by his life, teaching, death and resurrection Jesus raised humanity to a new level of union with the Divine - a spiritual evolutionary step. From what we know of the authentic words of Jesus, there is no indication that he understood the criminal's death as he foresaw to be his lot, as having a redemptive value, certainly not on behalf of all humanity. His death would inevitably follow on account of his pursuing against official religious opposition what he understood as his mission – to announce the new era (the Kingdom of God).

A redemptive interpretation of his death arose from the traumatic experience of his closest followers who, having had their great dreams of a new Messianic era - and their own important places in it - completely shattered within the space of a week following Jesus' triumphant entry into Jerusalem. As with all of us, suddenly faced with a horrifying or tragic death, some explanation had to be found. It is the only way we can cope with the disaster. They sought this in the prophecies of their Scriptures and in the context of the contemporary manner of appeasing God with Temple sacrifices. So we find in the Pauline letters repeated references to Jesus' 'sacrificial death' (Romans 5:9, Ephesians 2:13, 5:2, Colossians 1:20) as also in the Letter to the Hebrews (13:12, 20) and in other New Testament writings (Revelation 1:5, 5:9, 7:14, Acts 20:28) and many references to his dying on our behalf 'for our sins' (I Corinthians 7:23, II Corinthians 5:15, Galatians 1:4, 3:13, Ephesians 1:7, Hebrews 9:14-15).

HOW WAS THE CROSS REDEMPTIVE?

Throughout Christian history, while no doubt has been cast by believers upon the efficacy of Jesus' sacrifice on the cross for the redemption of all humanity, many theories have been put forward to explain HOW his death was redemptively effective. Explanations range from a transaction between God and humanity represented by Jesus, to a ransom being paid (to Satan?) to rescue us from the slavery of sin (I Corinthians 6:20 'He bought you for a price') to the theory of St Anselm of Canterbury (11th century) that satisfaction was made by Jesus on our behalf (a penal substitute), to Jesus as the scapegoat (Isaiah 53) the suffering servant taking God's anger upon himself.

If we look at Jesus' actions and parables we see he himself had quite a different understanding of how we are to be reconciled. He saw sin, not as a breaking of rules, of laws, but as a breakdown of relationships. Compensation to God was not required because it is God who takes the initiative. It is not something that humanity does for God. It is what God does for humanity. There are so many illustrations of Jesus' attitude to reconciliation:

Jesus eats with tax collectors and sinners without expecting them to confess their wrongdoing (Matthew 9:13).
The parable of the lost sheep (Matthew 18:12)
Peter asks should he forgive others who keep on offending him as many as seven times, to be told, not seven but seventy times seven – in other words every time (Matthew 18:21).
The parable of the unforgiving debtor (Matthew 18:23).
The paralytic lowered through the roof who had his sins gratuitously forgiven (Mark 2:1).
The sinful woman who anointed the feet of Jesus.

Her action proved that her many sins had already been forgiven (Luke 7:47).

The parable of the Prodigal Son (Luke 15:11).

The tax collector Zacchaeus promised restitution after he had been forgiven: forgiveness did not depend upon his making restitution (Luke 19:1).

The Good Thief on the cross did nothing to receive the promise of eternal life: it was gratuitous (Luke 23:39).

The woman caught in adultery was not to be punished. (John 8:1).

Today, for a variety of reasons, people feel uncomfortable with the traditional explanations of salvation. First, in our present culture, neither sacrifices nor slavery loom large. We do not think in terms of making sacrifices to appease God nor do we think of freedom in terms of being released from slavery. Secondly, the notion of sin has moved from being thought of as an offence against God to being considered more as an offence against our neighbour. Consequently it is to our neighbour we need to be reconciled rather than to God. Thirdly, all explanations of the need of salvation in the Christian tradition are based on the idea of the 'Fall' of humanity through Adam and Eve: a fall from a perfect state to a less perfect state. We now know that the Eden myth was a way of explaining our evolutionary step from non-differentiation (non-individuality) to differentiation (individuality). Fourthly, today we are more in control of our lives so we more willingly accept personal responsibility for our failings. Consequently, people feel less need of salvation. Fifthly, people feel that redemption is less about the 'after life': that the meaning of life is found in this world here and now. And sixthly, the action of Jesus 2000 years ago seems to many to be just too remote, irrelevant to our lives today.

Words like Redemption, Salvation, Atonement belong to another age and another culture. Ask people in the supermarket as evangelist missionaries do 'Are you saved?' and it is usually met with a black stare. We all want to be saved but it is from being in debt, from fear of a terrorist attack, from a natural disaster or even from unfriendly neighbours. In the case of the African people with whom I lived in villages, it was from ill health and witchcraft that they looked for deliverance. In other words, what concerns people of our time is not about saving their souls, nor about getting to Heaven but about the quality of their present lives. Is that such a bad thing in the light of the reason our 'Saviour' gave for why he had come: 'That you may have life, life in its fullness'?   (John 10:10). (I am not down-playing the value of the cross: it represents the acceptance of a path of non-violence.)

A FORWARD-LOOKING MISSION

In these words he was describing his mission not as backward looking - to undo a past Fall, to take us back to a previous Eden-state - but as forward-looking: as contributing to a gradual rise in human potential, an elevation to the potentials of Kingdom-living, empowering us to reach our total fulfilment.

To explain HOW what Jesus did 2000 years ago can affect us to-day, I draw upon the theory of Morphic Resonance proposed by the biochemist Rupert Sheldrake. He writes: 'The process by which the past becomes present within morphic fields is called Morphic Resonance. Morphic Resonance involves the transmission of formative causal influences through both space and time' (*The Presence of the Past*). For instance, once a particular obstacle to human endeavour has been overcome the ability to achieve the same is available to others of the same species through morphic fields which, unlike physical fields, are evolutionary.

The Guinness Book of Records has to be republished each year because people are continually breaking the barriers of physical human limitation, and, according to the theory of Morphic Resonance, thus empowering others to do the same. Here are just two well-known examples of this. For thousands of years people have been using a variety of boats to cross the English Channel. It was only in the 19th century that anyone succeeded in swimming across. That was Captain Webb in 1875. Since then literally hundreds of people have achieved the same, some now swimming there and back. A few years ago, Thomas Gregory, a twelve year old boy swam it. Furthermore, the swimmers are getting faster. Capt. Webb took 21 hours 45 minutes. Thomas Gregory took only 11 hours. The present record is held by a Californian girl who swam across in 7 hours 40 minutes. In 1991 Sussie Moroney from Australia swam to France and back in 17 hours. Again, no one had ever succeeded in reaching the summit of Mount Everest, despite many attempts, until it was reached by the New Zealander Edmund Hillary and his Sherpa guide Tenzing Norgay on 29th May 1953. Once the barrier to this particular human achievement had been broken, climbing Mount Everest has become an annual event. On May 10th 1993 forty reached the peak on the same day. In May 1998 Tom Whitaker reached the summit on his third attempt. He had lost a foot in a car accident nineteen years previously. In May 2000 a Nepalese Sherpa, Babu Chhiri, set a record for the fastest ascent – in 16 hours – more than four hours faster than the previous record holder and he used no extra oxygen.

To lift humanity out of its state of disharmony and to raise us to a higher state of spiritual evolution there needed to be one person who could break through the barrier of self-seeking and in doing so empower the whole of humanity to follow the same path. This is what Jesus did, as a completely fulfilled and enlightened human being, the most perfect icon of the Divine in human form. Through his total and unconditional love, being completely for the other, free of the inner enslavement to which we are all held captive, he opened up for humanity the possibility, indeed the ability, to live in the same way. Humanity was not thus empowered by receiving new gifts, but Jesus released on behalf of us all an untapped God-given gift: a creative energy to overcome our inherited selfishness.

JESUS SETS US FREE

When Salvation is understood in this way, it is interesting to compare the traditional notion of Jesus saving us as against the idea that Jesus set us free. Rather than Jesus saves us from the wrath of God he sets us free from a fear of God. He didn't save us by changing God's mind about us but by changing our mind about God. Not so much that he saved us from eternal separation from God but rather he set us free from the religious attitudes and practices that follow from a belief in separation.

REDEMPTION AS HEALING

We can apply the gift of Redemption to ourselves by understanding it not as forgiveness, but rather as the gift of a healing energy, an empowerment, so that 'we shall become mature people, reaching to the very height of the Christ's full stature' (Eph. 4:13). The healing, growth-giving energy is already ours as Potential Energy. It requires to be drawn upon. The work of natural healers - whether using Reflexology, Acupuncture, Reiki or any other method - is not to add anything to a person but to balance the life-giving energies we already possess so that they operate in harmony and so restore our bodily deficiencies. God's creative energy is a healing energy. Ancient cultures and schools of healing in China, India, Greece and Native America have long-recognised a life-force energy permeating, influencing and controlling our state of health. The healing power is in the exercise of energy at different levels: physical, emotional, psychic.

'I have come so that they may have life - life in all its fullness' (John 10:10). The Greek text uses the word *zoee* here (for life) which carries a sense of aliveness or physical energy, so: 'I have come so that they may have energy', the Divine Energy, Eternal Life.

Perhaps one of the most helpful descriptions of what Salvation, Redemption is all about is found in the letter to the Ephesians (3:16-19). (My interpretation of this passage is in brackets.)

'Out of his infinite glory, may God give you the power (the energy)

through his Spirit for your hidden (inner) self to grow strong, so that the Christ may live in your hearts (that you may be known as Christ) through faith,

and then, planted in love and built on love (the highest form of energy)

you will with all the saints

have strength to grasp the breadth and the length and the depth (the totality of the Cosmos),

until, knowing the love of the Christ, which is beyond all (intellectual) knowledge,

you are filled with the utter fullness of God (which is our final destiny).'

This is the offer: it calls for our response. It can only be applied as each person recognises the seeds of the Divine which is implanted in each of us. We are invited to tap into this potential energy. First, recognise it, as Jesus did in himself, then consciously tap into it by going deeper into ourselves, for which regular deep meditation is a key means.

10. OUR SPIRITUAL FUTURE

I have recently read a number of papers and articles in which the authors foresee that in the distant future all the world's religions will have coalesced to become one world religion.

While acknowledging that in recent decades the great religions have opened up a dialogue, unprecedented, and pledged to work together in the many areas which are of common concern – justice, peace, the preservation of family life, care for the environment – and although we hold so many values in common – love, honesty, mercy, selflessness, faithfulness, forgiveness, trustworthiness, sincerity, truthfulness – I personally do not see that one world religion to be on a distant horizon, however far away.

My own prognosis is that eventually – in another century maybe – all religions will have faded away and been replaced by a deep spirituality issuing from humanity's entering into a higher state of consciousness.

Before I go further, I must define my terms. During years of leading retreats, workshops, seminars on spirituality, I have asked participants to write down what they understand by the two words 'Spirituality' and 'Religion'. These are some of the views expressed about spirituality:

Getting in touch with the real self
Merging towards oneness with everything
Unconditional love
Finding a meaning in life
Asking: "Who am I?"
Being in touch with feelings
Compassion
To live your truth
Questing for one's higher self
Sensing the Divine
Moving towards the Absolute
Acknowledging one's own and others' divinity
Being in the present
The point of unity among humans
Harmony with all creation
Getting in touch with the essence of our nature
A return journey to our innocence
Being open to the Spirit
Cosmic interconnectedness
Connectedness with nature
Clearing the mind – opening the heart
Knowing how to relate to energy
A process of conscious evolution
A unity of everything that is in potential

Making a synthesis of these and many other answers I came up with the following:

Spirituality is that dimension of our nature – related to the physical and psychological dimensions – which awakens us to wonder, gives our lives meaning and calls us towards our higher self, usually expressed as a relationship with the Transcendent (sometimes called 'God').

The two elements that were most emphasised are first, that spirituality is related to having a meaning, a purpose, in life. Life itself has no purpose other than that which we give it. The major religions provide us with a purpose. But each of us has to make it our own. Without a purpose we can feel suicidal. Secondly, the sense of being drawn onwards by something beyond us. Nothing pleases us more than the feeling that we have grown a little, become more fulfilled, overcome one of life's hurdles. We all need to feel that this isn't it; there is more.

> *Religion* on the other hand, is a particular framework which includes four characteristics (a belief system, a moral code, an authority structure and a form of ritual) within which people find direction and nourishment for the spiritual dimension of their lives, and explore their spiritual journey in the company of others.

DRAWN BEYOND OURSELVES

In the Introduction I wrote of how, from the time our earliest ancestors became self-reflective creatures, they experienced a power beyond themselves. We, today, recognise this as their spirituality. This spiritual dimension was as much part of their humanity as the physical and intellectual dimensions. Indeed, spirituality is one of the ingredients that make us human beings different from all other creatures. It causes us to ask the most profound questions about life: Why are we here? What is our origin? What is our destination? Have we a destiny beyond this life?

The great religions, on the other hand, are very new-comers in human history. They developed to provide answers to those fundamental questions, but only over the last two and a half thousand years. In their origins, we can think of them as philosophies, ways of life, rather than religions.

We notice that spirituality, as part of our nature, is of concern to every person irrespective of any religious affiliation and is developed individually. A characteristic of religion, on the other hand, is that it is communal: people seeking together. We could say that as an element of our humanity spirituality is God-given while religion is a human creation.

So the world religions being of human origin, and so recent in our history, perform a transitory role in our development. They provide us with a framework, a support at this stage of our spiritual journey. A newly planted tree is tied to a pole to keep it straight and is fenced around to protect it in its earliest years. But then comes a time when the protection has to be removed to allow it to grow fully and expand. Not to remove the protection would cause it to be stifled in its growth. This is why I am projecting that the future will not see an amalgamation of religions but their giving way altogether to something beyond religion where the props of religion will no longer be necessary.

PRESENT TRENDS

However, this is in the very distant future and such a future is speculation. We need to earth ourselves, to look at the present and see if we can detect any trends in society by which we can recognise what might point to our future direction.

The Catholic Church, for instance, which until recent decades held firmly to the belief that 'outside the (Catholic) Church there is no salvation' has made a partial about-turn and now acknowledges that adherents of other religions can be saved, although it continues to explain that this is so through the redemptive act of Jesus the Christ, even though unknown to these people. It goes on to state that the redemptive graces are most fully available only through the Catholic Church!

'By their fruits you shall know them': the fruits of the Holy Spirit are evident and productive in persons and communities of other religions, and indeed the way in which they live their values can often put Christians to shame. Many see Buddhism as the most peace-loving and contemplative of all religions. Sikhism is a monotheistic religion which puts more emphasis on good practice in living than on creeds. Taoism can seem closer to the teaching of Jesus than does Christianity: a good Taoist has few needs and does not exercise power over others. Islam witnesses a regularity in prayer across the whole community which is an example to every Christian. Confucianism demonstrates a stronger commitment to the family, to the wider social unit and to good government than Christianity has ever been able to do. While we Christians continue to affirm that Jesus is truly divine and saviour, do we need to continue to insist that he alone is divine and saviour? Are we, as one theologian (Michel Foucault) suggests, always playing with power when we make assertions about what is really true?

All religions start with the premise that life is not as it should be: there is something wrong. This wrongness is variously called Original Sin, ignorance, evil or just suffering. Each religion offers an escape from this wrongness (named salvation or escape from the wheel of suffering, or enlightenment or Heaven) provided that that religion's particular 'way' is followed. Although the ways differ, there is so much we hold in common. The fact of 'God', transcendent and immanent (except in Buddhism). Our relationship to God as creature to Creator. That there is a spark of the Divine in all of us. However differently it is expressed, the Golden Rule – love your neighbour as yourself – is common to all the great religions. (See table in chapter 8)

Since all humanity has a common spiritual experience, although not a common interpretation of that experience, surely the only plausible way forward, is through an open non-self-serving dialogue between all Faiths, based upon what we have in common, so that together they serve the highest aspirations of the human person and the greatest good for the preservation of the world. A first step is to recognise religious pluralism. No one religion has all the truth, whatever their claims. Since for thousands of years the different religions have been a path for millions of people to develop their spiritual dimension, it cannot be denied that each must have a place in God's overall plan for humanity.

Similarly within Christianity. There are many paths to follow as a Christian. None can claim it is the one and only way. Each sees and emphasises different aspects of the truth. This has been happening throughout the Church's history.

After the Ascension, the Jerusalem community was led by James, the brother of Jesus. But soon the Gentile Christians, followers of St Paul, outnumbered them. After the fall of Jerusalem in CE 70 the Jerusalem Christians escaped to Pella in Jordan but by the end of the 5th century they had died out. When Paul announced the Good News around the Eastern Mediterranean, he let each community respond to it according to their culture, unlike the way in which later missionaries 'planted' the Church with a complete structure. Consequently, different forms of local Church emerged. Although a series of ecumenical councils were called to try and unify the growing Church, none succeeded completely. In fact they gave rise to three Christian paths, all of which still exist today. After the Council of Chalcedon in 451 Christians in Persia and China took a Nestorian path, while in Egypt and Ethiopia they chose the Coptic path. The rest of the then Christian world chose the path we in the West know today.

Then in 1054 there was the great schism between the western and eastern Churches. The Pope in Rome and the Patriarch of Constantinople excommunicated each other! In the 16th century there was the Protestant Reformation since when many Churches have continued to divide into many more, still today, most noticeably among the African Independent Churches.

Despite all the energy that has gone into the ecumenical movement over the last decades, the fact is that Christianity is likely to find even more diverse expressions in the years ahead.

THE NEW AGE

As churches empty, as people are less attracted to formal religion, as expressed in worship and creeds, so more are turning to matters spiritual, to give meaning to their lives. Out of this has grown the phenomenon labelled 'The New Age'. I have written at length on this subject in a previous book (*The Creative Christian*) so I will not repeat it all here, except to say that a lot of the features of the New Age are not new at all but are a bringing to the fore some very ancient practices.

What is of interest in our present context is why it is now, in our own times, that a spiritual revolution is taking place. I suggest that there are three features of today's life that *together* are causing a new expression of spirituality to emerge.

The first is an unease about the traditional concept of God. Bearing in mind that any image we have in our minds about God, any name we give to the Ultimate Reality is a human creation. God is the Reality that cannot be tied down by name. I wrote in an earlier chapter about the traditional idea of an interventionist God. Although people may still pray to God with the expectation that He will answer their prayers – even if the hoped for result is contrary to physical laws – at the same time they expect God to intervene to stop such horrors as the Holocaust and are surprised that He doesn't. Thinking of God simply as He who sits up there to supply our needs is no longer a mature adult's perception. Nor is the 'up there' God, as if existing in a separate box from the rest of life satisfying. The image of God as the law-giver who gave us 10 Commandments as a test of our worthiness for Heaven, God as our judge at the Last Day, God as He who inflicts punishment upon us, even eternal punishment in Hell – all these notions are speaking less to people of our day. So people are seeking a new perception of God that makes more sense to and relates to their everyday lives.

Secondly, as we mentioned above, people are now encountering other Faiths and appreciating the positive values of these Faiths and indeed how much their insights and practices can contribute to our own. Encountering people of other religions at the spiritual level they realise how much at that level we all share. That while religions divide humanity, spirituality unites us.

Thirdly, all the knowledge we have today through astrophysics of the utter vastness of our Universe gives us a new cosmology: a new big picture, a meta-story, to use New Age speak, of how almost inconspicuous we humans are in the total picture, we who once had the arrogance to think that the whole of creation was God's work just because ultimately He wanted human kind. That all the rest was simply a forerunner for our appearance. Isn't this the ultimate arrogance? And so this leads, as we have already said, to a move from super-nature theism to panentheism, appreciating God at work in our midst as the creative energy which sustains all and empowers our evolution.

But, we may ask, why is this new thinking, this move from traditional religion to a new spirituality, happening in our own time and not in our parents' time? One reason, I believe, is that official religions are not providing adequate or convincing answers to the questions being posed today. They are still vying with one another as to who possesses the fullness of truth. They are not offering the means to answer people's deep longing for a relevant spirituality. (How few Churches teach any form or method of contemplative meditation.)

Then there is the loss of faith in science, in technology, in reason to provide the ultimate answers to life as once they claimed to do – and often still do. Little wonder that today, in a time of post-modernism, there is the idea abroad that there is no such thing as objective truth. Things are understood, are judged, according to each one's perspective, each one's mental paradigm, which is continually changing as we are enriched with more knowledge and deeper experiences.

To these reasons we might add that we in the West live in a time of increased choice. We no longer accept that there is just one point of view, just one way of doing things, just one list of beliefs. We look around, judge each of the opportunities, see what appeals to us and end up with a pick-and-mix life and a pick-and-mix spirituality.

RETURNING TO JESUS

Many Christians, feeling dissatisfied with their Church membership as not furthering their spiritual journey and having abandoned the Church's doctrine, are turning once again to the person and message of Jesus of Nazareth. I closed the chapter on The Christ by mentioning how other world religions hold Jesus and his teaching in high regard, though not considering him to be an incarnation of God.

The kernel of Jesus' Good News is clothed in language about a kingdom: the Kingdom of God. Some people are put off by this metaphor, but we have to appreciate the historical background and Jewish culture of himself and his audience. What really drew the crowds to him was his personality and his authenticity. 'The crowd was amazed at what he taught. He wasn't like the teachers of the Law: instead he taught with authority' (Matthew 7:28-29). His power lay in his personal charisma. What he said – his parables about the Kingdom of God – simply explained the values by which he lived.

Although Jesus thought of himself as coming with a message for his fellow Jews only (Matthew 10:5-6, 15:24) there is no indication that he wished to found a new religion. The values he proposed by which humanity should live were not specific to his co-religionists but fundamental human values, applicable to every one of us. His vision transcends all races and cultures. He was not concerned with matters heavenly but with day-to-day life on Earth. This is why his person and his message, gleaned directly from the gospels and not as interpreted by the Church, are appealing to people of our day.

'I have come in order that you may have life – life in all its fullness' (John 10:10). What an appealing message to searchers for spirituality! No mention here of coming to make a blood sacrifice of himself to save the world. He referred to himself as 'the Way' (John 14:6) and his earliest followers were known as people of The Way.

In emphasising the divinity of Jesus, the Church has placed him beyond our reach, beyond being someone we can aspire to be like, a model, an ideal.

His unconditional love, the miracles he is reported to have worked – those of healing and those relating to the elements – he did, not because he was God but because he was a completely fulfilled, enlightened, human being – as fully evolved as it is possible for any person to be at our present stage of human evolution. We read of the same miracles being performed by very spiritually advanced gurus in India today. Jesus was not a super-human: he was totally human. It is we who are less than fully human. We should aspire to his state of humanity 'reaching to the very height of the Christ's full stature' (Ephesians 4:13).

AN INVITATION TO A NEW CONSCIOUSNESS

One of his sayings is so often misunderstood because it is mistranslated in English. The earliest account we have of his announcing a breakthrough to a new world order is given in Mark's gospel: 'The right time has come and the Kingdom of God is at hand. Repent and believe this Good News' (1:15). The word 'repent' is an unfortunate translation of the word *metanoia* in Greek, the language in which the gospel was written. It gives the impression that Jesus was saying 'express sorrow', 'be converted', 'make reparation', whereas *metanoia* has a much more profound meaning than that. Literally it means 'beyond the mind', just as 'metaphysics' means beyond, greater than the physical. What Jesus is saying is 'change your mind-set, put on a new mind' or as we might say today 'transcend your level of consciousness to understand this Good News'. Jesus expressed this in another way to the Jewish leader Nicodemus who crept to him for instruction by night. 'No one can see the Kingdom of God unless he is born again' (John 3;3). What Jesus is proposing as values for humanity to live by is that much different from our everyday level of consciousness, from our rational mind.

Is there any evidence that after two thousand years of proclaiming the Jesus message we can detect that humanity is moving any nearer living by the ideals that Jesus proposed? I believe we can, despite the negative picture of Planet Earth and the way we relate to it as continually presented by the media. I don't believe there is any more evil upon Earth today than there always has been. One has only to flip through the pages of a history book to see the appalling ways in which human beings treated one another in past centuries. As I wrote earlier, if there is an increase in evil abroad it is quantitatively more because there are more of us living on this planet now but it is not qualitatively worse. As we are faced with an apparent increase in the evidence of evil, so we can, if we look about us, see an increase in the outpouring of goodness. What is happening is a polarisation of both good and evil and this is a sign of the destruction there has to be of the old order so that the new order can come to birth. New life arises from the death of the old.

Already in 1964 the scientist and mystic Jesuit, Teilhard de Chardin, wrote:

A great many internal and external portents – political and social upheaval, moral and religious unease – have caused us all to feel, more or less confusedly, that something tremendous is at present taking place in the world. (*The Future of Man*).

Historians point out that civilisations go through a four-stage process of rise, growth, breakdown and disintegration. This is evidenced as occurring in the great civilisations of the last five thousand years: Egyptian, Syrian, Hellenic, Roman, Islamic, and more recently Christian and Western. The social symptoms are always the same: a sense of alienation, an increase in mental illness, violent crime, social disruption and an increased interest in religious cultism.

BREAKTHROUGH TO A NEW ERA

So against these too readily observable signs of breakdown, are there also signs of our breaking through to the kind of world which Jesus proclaimed as being the world God wants?

Throughout the book I have mentioned the emerging era of new consciousness. What Jesus says about changing our mind-set relates to this. But he also said at the end of his life that our knowledge of divine things would continue to increase. 'I have much more to tell you but now it would be too much for you to bear. When, however, the Spirit comes who reveals the truth about God, he will lead you into all the truth' (John 16:12-13).

Jesus also spoke about the re-awakening of the spiritual dimension of life. In his talk to the woman of Samaria by the well, he said: 'Believe me, the time will come when people will not worship the Father either on this mountain or in Jerusalem. ... But the time is coming and is already here, when by the power of God's Spirit, people will worship the Father as he really is, offering him the true worship that he wants. God is Spirit, and only by the power of his Spirit can people worship him as he really is' (John 3:21-24). And as he approached the end of his life he told his closest friends: 'I am telling you the truth: whoever believes in me will do what I do – yes, he will do even greater things' (John 14:12).

The Benedictine monk, Bede Griffiths, who developed an ashram in India wrote: 'I feel that we are on the eve of a new breakthrough in consciousness, of a new wave of civilisation'. (*Unpublished letter to H.W. December 22nd 1972*)

The word 'consciousness' is key to what our spiritual future is all about.

11. AN EMERGING CHRISTIANITY

In my introduction I raised a list of items that are questioning traditional Christian belief. That traditional Christianity is being challenged in a number of areas, but particularly in its expression of beliefs, is apparent from the statistics revealing a drop in church attendance of all the major Churches. (An exception is among the many evangelical literalist Churches, the reason for which will become apparent a little later.) One cannot help but notice the relationship between the dwindling number of people filling church benches on a Sunday and the increased number of books swelling the shelves of the Body, Mind and Spirit section of our bookshops. I do not interpret this as a disillusionment with Christianity, but as a disillusionment with the Church and a search for a more relevant way of being a Christian.

Let us begin by having a close look at what is actually happening among Christians in the West today. I have already spoken of the shift of consciousness taking place in the human population in our times, to a new understanding of reality – a new paradigm – and this is affecting Christians as much as others.

I propose for consideration that there is emerging a different way of being a Christian in our time. I refrain from calling it a 'new' form of Christianity because we cannot re-invent Christianity any more than we can re-

invent Jesus the Christ, despite the fact that attempts
have been made in past times to re-invent the personality of Jesus: I'm thinking of the 'Gentle Jesus meek
and mild' portrait.

A MOVEMENT INWARDS

What is happening, I believe, is that Christianity is
taking a different direction, going inwards, from being
outwards. More concerned with the way we live than
with what we believe. This is what accounts for less
interest in public worship and more interest in such
inner practices as deep meditation. It is actually
returning to the core of the Good News of Jesus,
understanding what the Jesus event was all about.
And what can be more Christian than that?

Let me explain. The picture becomes clearer if I
label the fading traditional form of Christianity 'Outer
Christianity' and the emerging form as 'Inner
Christianity': Christianity with a soul. Clearly no
expression of Christianity is completely one or the
other but I recognise an increasing trend from the
former to the latter.

It would be wrong to label the former 'old' and the
latter 'new' because the shift to inner Christianity is
actually a return to the heart of the Good News and
was the predominant form of Christianity for
centuries.

I have for long been puzzled why Christianity,
unlike all the other great religions, insists more on
orthodoxy, the right belief, than on the way we live.
Judaism is primarily about following the 'way of
Torah'. Central to Buddhism is the practice of the
'eightfold path'. Of the Moslems' five pillars of Islam,
four are about practice. Indeed, the Bible, the New

Testament in particular, and Jesus himself, were more concerned about our life's values and how we live up to them than about adhering to a set of beliefs. I ascribed this insistence on belief in certain truths to the fact that the other world religions are more culturally related - Hinduism and Buddhism with India, Taoism and Confucianism with the Far East, Islam with the Middle East, Judaism with its own historical culture - while Christianity being worldwide had to have some way of deciding who was in and who was out, who belonged and who did not. This was assessed by a list of beliefs - forms of which are the Apostles' and Nicene creeds - which a member is required to tick off. An obvious example of this process is the list of beliefs which a Church has to acknowledge if it is applying for membership of the World Council of Churches.

However, I believe there are two historical events in western history which have emphasised the need for correct belief. The first was the Reformation, which caused the Protestant and Catholic Churches to draw up their battle lines in the trenches of what each considered to be Christian truth. There was an emphasis on the Protestant side of our being saved by faith not by works. Then there was the Church's fear of the challenge of the Enlightenment, of the 17th century, which emphasised the power of the reasoning mind to replace divine revelation as the source of knowledge about the great questions of life. And came with it the birth of science as we know it and the opening up of today's scientific knowledge which has transformed our western culture. The need for religious belief was strengthened as a defence against the emerging Enlightenment, and one cannot help wondering whether there was also, as an undercurrent, an element of fear on behalf of Church leaders of losing control.

This seems to be the point at which theological thinking got fossilised and began to fall behind the developing thought of other disciplines. The theologian Bernard Lonergan expressed the view that Catholic theology began to fall behind the times around 1680: 'When modern science began, when the Enlightenment began, then theologians began to reassure one another about their certainties' (*Theology in its New Context*).

Church leaders are not the only ones who fear losing control through a variety of beliefs. Back in the 4th century the Emperor Constantine summoned the Bishops to a Council in Nicaea in 325, at which he presided, directing them to come up with a statement of beliefs with which they were all in agreement - they gave us the Nicene Creed - because he feared that the variety of beliefs in local Churches, especially over the Arian controversy, was divisive in his empire.

TRUTH OR HERESY

Whenever divergent views reared their heads, Church authorities had to decide between what they regarded as truth - the one and only truth - and heresy. They had to decide, for instance, which books of Scripture they understood to be inspired, and so included in our Bibles, and which should be dropped. (Protestant, Anglican, Catholic and Orthodox Churches still have different opinions on this question today.)

And yet having a blind unreasoning faith in what is proposed for Christian belief has never been expected. In the Middle Ages the great theologian St Thomas Aquinas wrote in his Summa: 'People cannot give consent in faith to what is proposed to them unless to some extent they understand it' (11-11,q.8,a.8,ad.2).

I believe that what is happening among Christians in the West today is not simply a development of ideas, a questioning of truth proposed. It is more fundamental than that. There is a new Christian paradigm emerging.

There are various descriptions of a paradigm, but put simply, I understand it as our mental framework for perceiving, thinking, valuing and doing based upon a particular vision of reality. We see the world and make our judgments through the lens of our paradigm. Three examples will illustrate this. There was a shift in paradigm in the 16th century from a Ptolemaic view that the Earth was the centre of creation, around which the Sun span, to the Copernican Universe which placed the Sun as the centre of our astrological system. So dramatic was this, so against the biblical interpretation of that time, that popular opinion and immediate observation (of a rising and setting Sun) were all against the proposition.

The second example of a paradigm shift is from the Creationist to the Evolutionist account of the origins of life and explanation of living forms, the latter supported by the discovery of numerous fossil remains and the similarity of the DNA codes in all forms of living creatures.

Nearer our own time (20th-century) is the paradigm shift from a Newtonian physics (proposed in the 17th century) of a mechanistic materialist Universe to our present Quantum Physics, understanding the Universe in terms of energy. Although it must be said that most people still remain committed in everyday life to the

Newtonian view if only because it is more easy to imagine.

FROM HEAD TO HEART

I am proposing that today we are seeing a paradigm shift from a belief-centred Christianity to an experience-centred Christianity. From head to heart.

Belief-centred Christianity is more concerned with right belief and observance of what that belief requires. For example, as I mentioned in my introduction, belief in an interventionist God requires that we worship Him, that we behave in such a way as to earn a heavenly reward, or at least avoid offending Him so grievously that we might be despatched to Hell for all eternity. Further, we have to believe that He intervened at a certain point in human history by sending His Son Jesus to die on a cross to redeem us from our fallen state and that Jesus is thus the only means of salvation for all humanity and that in consequence of which Christianity is the only true religion, by which is implied that all the other religious paths are false and so lead to perdition. This paradigm stresses our sinfulness, causes an emphasis on guilt and consequently of the need of forgiveness, all of which feature largely in Church worship.

I mentioned earlier that the one exception to the emptying churches are those evangelical churches which preach a literal understanding of the Bible. These are supported by Christians who are feeling threatened, insecure in light of the emerging form of Christianity and wish for an unchanging, safe faith upon which to rely to assure their eternal salvation.

I don't believe we in the West are less spiritual today than we ever were. On the contrary, as the traditional Christian paradigm grows in disfavour people are searching more for a spiritual dimension to their lives. This is what is giving rise to what I am calling an Inner Christianity, less concerned with public ritual, more with spiritual experience.

Perhaps I could express the difference between the two Christian paradigms in this way. The traditional form is concerned with what we do for God and what God does for us: obeying His laws, winning His favour, worshipping Him, believing His revealed truths correctly and so winning our eternal reward. The emerging Christian paradigm is concerned with co-operating with God active in creation, partnering God in His concern for our quality of life on this Earth. The former relates to God as father, the latter to God as friend.

Finally, I believe this paradigm shift is coming about within the context of humanity entering a new evolutionary stage. There are signs aplenty, if we are aware enough to recognise them, that we are emerging from the stage of *Homo sapiens* to what is sometimes called *Homo luminus*, or *Homo spiritus*, having the ability to perceive at a much higher level of consciousness the vibrations and psychic energies that make up our physical world.

Unlike previous evolutionary stages of living creatures which have produced us human beings through a progression of natural, physical stages, this emerging step, precisely because it is a development of consciousness is of a different nature. It can only be brought about wilfully through the expanding human consciousness of self-conscious creatures: through humanity deliberately taking the next step. One sign of this evolution, and indeed one contribution towards it, is what I am calling the emerging inner Christianity.

12. THE HUMAN FUTURE

My knowledge is pessimistic, but my willing and
hoping are optimistic.
(Albert Schweitzer)

To name one of the characteristics of our times we have
coined the word 'Globalisation'. In most people's
minds the word has a negative connotation because the
concept is limited to Economic Globalisation. There are
many reasons for giving it this negative value, when
we think of the economic power, which gives political
power, through the domination of world markets by
trans-national companies whose budgets are greater
than the national budgets of many developing
countries. We think of terrorism which is now on a
global scale, of mass migration and of people-
trafficking, of the world-wide unrestricted trade in
armaments. And so the list could go on.

Globalisation is the present stage in a process that is
as long as human history. A process of human beings
being attracted to ever-larger groupings. From clan to
tribe, to villages, to towns, to cities, to nations, to
empires. Now empires have gone. Nation states are
going, metropolises are expanding and international
unions are forming: the United Nations, the European
Union, the Africa Union. We now speak of our world
as the Global Village.

This drawing together reveals the positive aspects of

globalisation. To name a few: the easy encounter with other races through cheap travel to distant countries or through their becoming our neighbours in our own country. We are coming to appreciate the values of other religions and what these can contribute to our own. We now enjoy a wide variety of exotic menus in the increasing choice of different ethnic restaurants.

Every type of fruit and vegetable is available all year round in our supermarkets. (I am making no judgement about the pollution to the atmosphere caused by transporting all these exotic foods!) We have no further need to travel to libraries – even specialist libraries in distant towns – to seek the information we need. It is available at the tap of a key on our computer thanks to the Internet. We receive instantaneous news of disasters in far-off places – in countries we may never even have heard of – and we reach for our cheque books to respond. We have come to have a greater sense of the oneness of humanity and of our responsibility for it.

I believe there is no such thing as chance. Each of us is here at this particular time, in this place, with these relationships to other people and to our environment, in these circumstances, for a purpose. We are each part - a contributing part - of the unfolding drama of evolution. Everything in the Universe is perpetually in movement. It is going somewhere though we know not where. Only our religious faith can answer that. But every faith tells us we are called to play our part, and that collectively.

WE CREATE OUR OWN REALITY

The theoretical physicist, Werner Heisenberg, in the mid-1920s was able to demonstrate that an observer, by the choices she or he made, was able to influence the outcome of a physical experiment. We are not simply observing the world 'out there' by our observation, we are actually creating what we see through the act of observation. The explanation lies in Quantum Physics. Physicists have come to realise that all is quantum energy existing in either waves or particles. Waves are full of possibilities. When consciousness is applied to the wave, by being observed, it is actualised as a particle. It takes form.

Einstein said: 'Everything is made of emptiness and form is condensed emptiness.' In the East they knew this 2,500 years ago. The Buddhist Heart Sutra states: 'Form is none other than emptiness and emptiness is none other than form'. Physical and non-physical reality are the same. What we perceive as wide open space is composed of the same particles and waves as objects we perceive as physical.

On a somewhat larger scale, a consciousness is necessary to materialise the Universe. We name that Supreme Consciousness God. Which is why we can say 'We are all but a thought in the mind of God'. When mystics say: 'All is God' they might as easily say: 'All is consciousness'. There is just one consciousness in which we all share. Each of us is the centre of the Universe - not only spatially because there is no top, bottom, left or right - but because each of us gives it meaning.

In dealing with concepts of such vastness it is helpful to have some form of imagery. Thomas Huxley (1825-95) a foremost supporter of Charles Darwin's theory of evolution (who in tackling Bishop Samuel Wilberforce on evolution famously declared that he would rather be descended from an ape than a Bishop!)

envisaged the Universe as a game of chess. The rules of the game were the laws of nature, the pieces represented the physical systems and the game itself the evolution of the Universe. God, so to speak, sets the rules, but the rules do not determine the outcome of the game. The players freely move the game forward by their foresight and ingenuity. So the game becomes an exquisite mix of order and unpredictability. In this imagery, God never needs to intervene to suspend or manipulate or bend His own laws and there is room for human freedom, including the chance operating at quantum or chaos level.

I prefer the simile of a wheel. God is at the centre, at the still point of a revolving wheel at which point there is neither space nor time, but the wheel revolves around it . We are on the circumference, in movement, in space, in time. God does not foresee the future nor see the past because at the centre past and future are one. At the centre all just is. It is the perpetual NOW. We are in movement, learning from our past, contributing to our future but all the time in relation to the centre - at the same distance to the still point, to God in His is-ness.

How often we hear it said: 'It's all in the mind'. What hangs on the wall in an art gallery is seen as a painting, not by the eyes, but by the mind which sorts out the lights that enter through the eyes. We see the picture in our head, not hanging on the wall. We create our own sadness, anxiety, depression as equally we can create our joy, happiness, pleasure. Everything - thoughts, feelings, emotions, sensations, associations - is an expression of energy, an expression we create.

We see other people as we wish to see them. We interpret events as we wish to understand them. When we believe something we feel it is true. It becomes true for us. Things that happened to us are interpreted by that belief system. We believe the reality we create is the true one. It follows that old beliefs need to be looked at and deconstructed or reconstructed in our present paradigm if they are to have a value for our lives at this moment.

IT IS UP TO US

So, collectively we have an enormous responsibility for the direction evolution takes. This applies to us individually. Every thought, idea, wish, every activity of the brain generates an electric impulse. It is creative. But our responsibility is also collective. I cannot claim ever to have been to a professional football match but I am told that the chances of a home team winning are greater than for a visiting team. Why? Because more of the home team fans are present - all expressing, with great and vehement solidarity, their desire for the home team to win. They collectively generate an energy which transfers to the players. How can this happen? Because all of us are different manifestations of the same essence in the field of consciousness. We are all interconnected through our common consciousness. 'Consciousness is a singular of which the plural is unknown'. (Ervin Schroedinger).

Quantum theory also demonstrates our interconnectedness in the physical realm. In ways we cannot perceive, neutrinos – fundamental particles - move in and out of us. These are the basic building blocks of life in people, animals, plants, as they are of rocks. Elements of everything in creation move through us and around us so that we can truly say a part of you is a part of me. We are all part of each other. We are all one, one with the One who creates the Universe.

Over the years of directing retreats I have made the point that what Jesus was saying by 'Love your neighbour as yourself' was 'Love your neighbour as you love yourself'. So, I would preach, and if we were to have a true appreciation of our neighbour, it must follow from a true appreciation of ourselves. It had to begin with our loving ourselves as the beautiful creation of God that we are. (My favourite verse in the psalms is: 'I thank you for the wonder of my being' [Psalm 139].)

But now I have come to realise that I was misinterpreting what Jesus actually said. We have to understand his words literally: 'Love your neighbour as yourself'. We are all one: one in divine essence. As Jesus said: 'I am in the Father and the Father is in me' (John 14:10), so I am in my neighbour and my neighbour is in me. We are to love our neighbour because our neighbour and ourselves are one. I am but one manifestation of the Divine as my neighbour is another manifestation of the same Divine. Jesus said of a child: 'Whoever welcomes in my name one of these children, welcomes me; and whoever welcomes me, welcomes not only me but also the one who sent me' (Mark 9:37). Now I understand why Jesus prayed to God for his followers: 'That you may be one just as you and I are one' (John 17: 11). And again: 'I pray that they all may be one' (John 17:21). We are all the same reality – reflections of the Ultimate Reality - but differently expressed.

This has given me quite a new meaning of: 'Love your neighbour as yourself'.

What will be the next stage of our evolution? What is humanity's future? I suggest it will be a uniting of humanity, not simply at the knowledge level, but at the heart level, at the level of a deeper consciousness. Jesus did say to his followers: 'When that day comes, you will know that I am in my Father and that you are in me, just as I am in you' (John 14:20).

WE ARE ARTISANS OF OUR FUTURE

When we were young we dreamt dreams. We would put the world to rights. We believed it was within our capacity to do so. We had ideals. Now in our adulthood we can appreciate the potential we have to improve the human situation, however local that might be. We are all artisans of our future.

The myriad problems with which humanity is faced – and we can be forgiven for believing that they are increasing in number and perplexity – will never be solved without a change in consciousness. Einstein said: 'We cannot solve a problem at the same level of consciousness that created it'. We will not solve the threat of terrorism by the might of armies. We will not overcome world poverty by adjusting the international trade rules. It is not an economic problem, it is a willingness problem. This planet produces enough food for all six and a half billion of us, but we do not have the will to share it. We cannot change the problem of youth violence in our streets by sending the offenders to gaol. These and so many more problems will only be solved by approaching them at a different level of consciousness. An example of this happening was in setting up the Truth and Reconciliation Commission in South Africa to draw the apartheid era to a close.

Solving the world's problems through a higher level of consciousness requires tapping the highest level of energy: love. Love is the universal language. There is not a person who is not touched by love: by a look, a touch, a smile, a kindly act. Love is the deepest form of communication. Its language is silence, its expression is sharing. 'There is no fear in love; perfect love drives out all fear' (I John 4:18). Love lived, experienced, recognised, alone can bring peace and unity to humanity. Love is the realm of the mystics.

Karl Rahner, the prominent Catholic theologian of the late 20th century wrote in *The Spirituality of the Church of the Future*: 'The Christian of the future will be a mystic or he will not exist at all.' I would say this is true, not just of the Christian, but of every person. What did he mean by ' a mystic'?

The word 'mysticism' is associated with mystery. It means to see beyond the physical reality: to see the presence of the Divine in everyone and everything around. To be able to appreciate that in the diversity of humanity – cultures, traditions, religions – lies the creative energy of God, the same energy we all share. This starts with our recognising and respecting the Divinity within ourselves.

To be a mystic means to live from the heart, to be centred, to be whole. It means appreciating what we consider to be the feminine values: emotions, feelings, imagination, intuition. Everyone of us is called to be a mystic.

One of the means that more and more people are adopting today, the practical means they are taking to follow this path, is through a discipline of some twice-daily form of deep meditation. Being a holistic exercise it gives nourishment and balance to those three dimensions of our lives: body, mind and spirit, as St Paul names them (I Thessalonians 5:23). Unless one is integrated within, one's energies are not unified and one is unable to receive and cooperate with the inner work of God's creative Spirit.

All the different methods, techniques of meditation on offer, have the same purpose: to still our busy minds. To allow us to be attentive to the Spirit within. The famous mystic of the Middle Ages, Meister Eckhart wrote: 'Nothing in all creation is so like God as stillness'. It is a way of journeying to the still centre of the wheel, to be in touch with the eternal NOW, the only Reality.

In the chapter on 'Tapping the Divine Energy' I spoke of the power emanating from a group of people meditating together, to lower the stress level – the cause of so much violence – of a neighbourhood. This is even more powerful than the energy generated by the fans of the home team at a football match.

SYNERGY

The greater the number of people meditating together, the more powerful and widespread their effectiveness. There are several organisations which invite people to pray or meditate for peace at a specific time on a certain date, so as to form a critical mass. One such is the Planetary Commission for Global Healing, based in Texas, which designates December 31st each year as World Healing Day for 'a global mind link, the purpose of which is to reverse the polarity of the negative force field' through achieving ' a critical mass of spiritual consciousness and so usher in a new era of peace on Earth'. Their first event was in 1986 when 'the mind-link totalled more than 500 million people representing all religious faiths on seven continents' encompassing all time zones during the twenty-four hour period. The event picks up greater numbers each year. The organisers describe the event as: 'A moment of Oneness to dissolve the separation and return humankind to Godkind'.

A similar organisation is Operation Planet Love operating out of Mexico. They select 25 days and particular GMT hours at which all participants are asked to pray for at least 21 minutes. The chosen days have a special significance, for example, the Equinox and Solstice, International Day of Peace (3rd Tuesday of September), All Saints Day (1st November).

Cynics might say: it is not noticeable this makes any difference. We need to reply: would our world have been worse without? The effect of these events cannot be measured.

However, what is true of good must, on the same basis, be true of evil. In biblical times natural disasters were attributed to human misdeeds on a tribal scale, interpreted as an act of a punishing God. As I write we are continually hearing news bulletins about tribal factions, international wars, racial pogroms and ethnic battles the length and breadth of the African continent? Is it entirely fanciful to suppose that there might be a connection between so much violence, bloodshed, hate and negativity in the human consciousness of millions of people and the climatic conditions causing floods, droughts, earthquakes – what we might call cosmic violence? We all influence the energies around us. As I write there is an unprecedented famine caused by drought in Sudan, a country in which there has been war between the Moslems in the North and the Christians and traditional religionists in the South for the last twenty years.

The parable of Noah and the Ark is a warning that

when a people do evil, the weather strikes back, not because God intervenes to punish us but because our negativity affects the balance of nature.

The alarming fact is that since we developed the atomic bomb in 1945 we human beings have seized from God control of our planet. Today it is we, not God, who decide whether to maintain it in its evolutionary path or whether to destroy all humanity and the planet in one mighty explosion. 'What terrifies me is not the explosive power of the atomic bomb, but the power of wickedness of the human heart' (Einstein).

But thinking positively, the coming evolutionary development is not a physical stride as in the past – from inorganic to plant to animal to human - but a step into a higher consciousness and this will only come about when we creatures with our self-reflective consciousness choose to bring it about. Surely the time is now. It all depends upon you and me.

Nobody made a greater mistake than he who did nothing because he could only do a little. (Edmund Burke)

CONCLUSION

In the chapter on God I made the important distinction, made by Meister Eckhart, between the *Godhead* (that is God unmanifest, beyond our comprehension) and *God* manifest, the image we create in order to have a relationship with the Divine.

I have proposed that a manner of perceiving God, which is more acceptable to our scientific age thinking, is of God manifest as creative energy, acting within creation (panentheism), thus allowing us to acquire a new kind of relationship with God, rather than imagining God as a superlative human being intervening from outside creation. Each one of us is part of that creation. As part, we are not a collection of human beings, we are *being* appearing as humanity. Our being is the material expression of Divine Being. We are each (somewhat imperfectly) a mirror of God. Our life force is Divine energy.

Having another look at the diagram we saw previously, we can see how the Godhead belongs to the metaphysical realm, what I am now calling the Fifth dimension (space-time being the Fourth), whereas our created image of God belongs to the physical, the realm of intellect. The speed of light is the physical barrier between the two.

Although we live in both realms, we are more conscious of the physical realm because it is in that that we operate our daily business. We can relate to

THE REALM OF THE GODHEAD

THE REALM OF SPIRIT - the Metaphysical -the Paranormal
The state of transcendence - The unified field of
consciousness
THE FIFTH DIMENSION

> No mass
> No space-time
> The eternal NOW - timeless
> Formless
> Immeasurable
> Unknowable to our five senses
> Realm of intuition, of mysticism

above
==================================*speed of light*
below

THE REALM OF OUR PERCEPTION OF GOD

THE PHYSICAL UNIVERSE - the normal

> Positive energy
> Positive mass
> Positive space-time
> Gravity bound
> Having form
> Measurable
> Knowable to the senses
> Realm of the intellect

We live in both worlds though we are not often aware of the Fifth
dimension. However there is among us a growing awareness of it.

the Godhead in the metaphysical realm, not by prayer of words but through deep contemplative meditation, which draws us into the state of transcendence.

There is evidence aplenty that a new spirituality is breaking through today, that there is a real shift of consciousness taking place whereby more and more people are becoming aware how the realm of Spirit is touching their lives, and this, often outside any religious practice on their part. They are experiencing that they are in tune with the Fifth dimension.

If our present world is to be saved from chaos - from extinction even – it is imperative that this awareness increases among us. We must trust our own experience of the Fifth dimension as it responds to the Fifth dimension of the reality around us. Dr Robert Muller, former Deputy Director General of the United Nations wrote : 'Either the twenty-first century will be a spiritual century or there will be no century at all'.

Ursula King, writing on the spirituality of Teilhard de Chardin (*Christ in All Things*) wrote:

The only subject ultimately capable of mystical transfiguration is the whole of humankind forming a single body and a single soul in charity. In his essay 'The Spirit of the Earth' (1931) this great vision of one world and one human community is once again strongly expressed. If we wish to extend rather than diminish our capacity of being human, we have to draw on the 'incredible power of love,' 'the primal and universal psychic energy,' 'the most universal, the most tremendous and the most mysterious of the cosmic forces'. For Teilhard, love is 'a sacred reserve of energy; it is like the blood of spiritual evolution' through which we can develop

the sense of the earth and 'the miracle of a common
soul' for the world.

SOURCES

Aron, E & A. (1986) *The Maharish Effect,* Stillpoint Publishing, New Hampshire, USA.

Barrow, John D (1992) *Theories of Everything,* Vintage, London.

Baum, Gregory. (1970) *Man Becoming,* Herder & Herder, New York

Berry, Thomas (1988) *The Dream of the Earth,* Sierra Club, San Francisco

Braden, Gregg (2004) *The Isaiah Effect.* Hay House Inc. London

Coats, Callum (1996) *Living Energies,* Gateway Books, Bath

Davies, Paul (1992) *The Mind of God,* Simon & Schuster, Ltd, London

De Chardin, Teilhard. (1964) *The Future of Man,* Collins, London (1969) *Human Energy.* Collins, London

Dossey, Larry (1993) *Healing Words.* Harper, San Francisco

Goswami, Amit. (1993) *The Self-Aware Universe,* Simon & Schuster, London (2001) *The Physics of the Soul.* Hampton Roads Publishing, USA

Hawkins, David (2000) *Power vs. Force.* Veritas Publishing, Arizona, USA

Hick, John. (1993) *God and the Universe of Faiths,* Oneworld Publications, NY, USA
- (1999) *The Fifth Dimension,* Oneworld Publications, Boston, USA

Hitchcock, John (1991) *The Web of the Universe,* Paulist

Press, Mahwah, NJ, USA

King, Ursula, (1997) *Christ in All Things* SCM Press, London.

Laszlo, Ervin (2004) *Science and the Akashic Field,* Inner Traditions, Rochester, Vermont, USA

Lorimer, David (1990) *Whole in One,* Arkana, London

McTaggart, Lynne (2001) *The Field,* Element, London

Maharishi International University (1990) *The Maharishi Effect.* MIU Press, Fairfield, Iowa, USA

Mooney, Christopher F. (1966) *Teilhard de Chardin & the Mystery of Christ.* Collins, London

Panikkar, Raimundo. (1964) *The Unknown Christ of Hinduism.* Darton, Longman & Todd, London.

Peacocke, Arthur (2004) Essay in *In Whom We Live and Move and Have our Being,* Philip Clayton & Arthur Peacocke, eds. Wm. B. Eerdmans Publ. Co. Cambridge

Playfair, Guy L. (2002) *Twin Telepathy: The Psychic Connection.* Vega, USA

Sheldrake, Rupert (1985) *A new Science of Life,* Paladin Books, London

- (1989) *The Presence of the Past,* Fontana Collins, London

- (1999) *Dogs that Know when their Owners are Coming Home,* Hutchinson, London

Smith, Adrian (2004) *The God Shift,* The Liffey Press, Dublin

Wilkinson, David (1993) *God, The Big Bang and Stephen Hawking,* Monarch, Tunbridge Wells, UK

BOOKS

O books

O is a symbol of the world, of oneness and unity. In different cultures it also means the "eye", symbolizing knowledge and insight, and in Old English it means "place of love or home". O books explores the many paths of understanding which different traditions have developed down the ages, particularly those today that express respect for the planet and all of life.

For more information on the full list of over 300 titles please visit our website
www.O-books.net

SOME RECENT O BOOKS

The Creative Christian God and Us; Partners in Creation
Adrian B. Smith

This book is a real appetite-whetter in its great scope and clarity. It succinctly gathers together the process and development of Science, Religion and Spirituality. Most importantly, it identifies the deep shifts in perspective that are taking place as we move towards globalisation. A truly inspirational vision for now and the future.
Mary Jo Radcliffe Chair of The Guild of Pastoral Psychology and founder of "Coping with Change"
1905047754   144pp **£11.99 $24.95**

A Global Guide to Interfaith
Reflections From Around the World
Sandy Bharat

This amazing book gives a wonderful picture of the variety and excitement of this journey of discovery.
Rev Dr. Marcus Braybrooke, President of the World Congress of Faiths
1905047975   336pp **£19.99 $34.95**

Bringing God Back to Earth
John Hunt
Knowledgeable in theology, philosophy, science and history. Time and again it is remarkable how he brings the important issues into relation with one another... thought provoking in almost every sentence, difficult to put down.
Faith and Freedom
1903816815   320pp **£9.99 $14.95**

From the Bottom of the Pond
The forgotten art of experiencing God in the depths of the present moment
Simon Small

Don't just pick this book up, read it and read it again. It's the best Christian book I have read in years. This is a book that will inform, delight, and teach. It needs to be heard. It has the potential to light up Christianity. This is what happens when God is happening. It's a brave book, expressing what it feels like to feel God. It shines a light on God in the midst of life, in the detail and the dirt, and it should be on every Christian's reading list.

Revd Peter Owen-Jones, Anglican Priest, author and BBC TV presenter of The Lost Gospels and The Battle for Britain's Soul.
9781846940   96pp **£7.99 $16.95**

God Without God
Western Spirituality Without the Wrathful King
Michael Hampson

Writing with an admirable lucidity and following a tight line of argument, Michael Hampson outlines a credible Christian theology for the twenty-first century. Critical at times of both evangelical and catholic traditions, of both liberal and conservative thinking, he seeks to make faith accessible to those for whom established forms of belief have become inappropriate in the present-day context.

Canon David Peacock, former Pro-Rector, University of Surrey
9781846941023   256pp **£9.99 $19.95**

Gospel of Falling Down
The beauty of failure, in an age of success
Mark Townsend

It's amazing just how far I was drawn into Mark's words. This wasn't just a book but an experience. I never realized that failure could be a creative process.
Editor, *'Voila'* Magazine
1846940095 144pp £9.99 $16.95

Let the Bible Be Itself
Learning to read it right
Ray Vincent

An honest book about what the Bible is and is not! Vincent exposes why millions of people misuse the Bible and cause havoc with it. All this is laid bare and a different, positive view of the Bible is offered to replace it. A necessary and excellent book!
Adrian Thatcher, Professorial Research Fellow in Applied Theology at the University of Exeter, UK
9781846941481 160pp £11.99 $24.95

The Monster God
Coming to Terms with the Dark Side of Divinity
John Mabry

The God of anger and judgment has been with us since the dawn of time, and surfaces widely today in the theology and experience of believers of all kinds of faith. This personal memoir provides a reflective, easy to read theological and philosophical analysis of how this god came to haunt our collective imaginations, how we can come to terms with him and where we go from here.
9781846940842 192pp £9.99 $19.95